GETTING INTO THE UK'S BEST UNIVERSITIES & COURSES

2ND EDITION

Susanne Christian

1 1 2 9 6 8

Getting into the UK's Best Universities & Courses

This second edition published in 2011 by Trotman, an imprint of Crimson
Publishing, Westminster House, Kew Road, Richmond, Surrey TW9 2ND
First edition published in 2008 by Trotman Publishing.

Author: Susanne Christian
Author of the first edition: Beryl Dixon

ISBN: 978 1 84455 396 9

British Library Cataloguing in Publication Data
A catalogue record for this book is available from the British Library

Typeset by RefineCatch Ltd, Bungay, Suffolk
Designed by Andy Prior
Printed and bound by LegoPrint SpA, Trento

GETTING INTO THE UK'S BEST UNIVERSITIES & COURSES

Contents

ABOUT THE AUTHOR

Susanne Christian is a qualified and experienced careers adviser who has worked for the Connexions service in schools, colleges and the community. She has written careers books and contributed to careers websites. Now self-employed, Susanne works as a career coach and employability tutor with all ages, helping people to explore their options, including moving into higher education.

Susanne can be contacted at susannechristian24@gmail.com.

ACKNOWLEDGEMENTS

As well as the young people and higher education institution staff who helped me, I would like to thank Ian Jack of the University of Liverpool, Corinne Lewis of Liverpool Institute of Performing Arts and Amanda Lovejoy of North London Collegiate School.

INTRODUCTION

This book is written for school and college students who are starting to think about higher education (HE). You are likely to be in Year 12 or 13 (sometimes called lower and upper sixth) or S5 or S6 in Scotland. Or perhaps you're doing a post-16 vocational course at college. If you are in a lower year, this book is still for you too – and well done for starting to think about higher education in good time.

There are a lot of references in this book to UCAS. If you have started thinking about applications for higher education or you have friends, sisters or brothers who have been through the process you will have heard of UCAS. You may not know that these initials stand for the Universities and Colleges Admissions Service. If you are not familiar with UCAS, you will need to get to know about it, as it is the organisation which handles the vast majority of applications for higher education in the UK. Take a look at the website www.ucas.com. More details about UCAS can be found in Chapter 2 – and throughout the book.

This book is not a magic guide to getting into any particular university or college. There are no special tricks, as you will realise every time the press comes up with another story about a star student who has been denied a place at an excellent university; or, as happened in the summer of 2010, when nearly 180,000 applicants failed to get a university place after the A level results were published, despite many of them being awarded the new A* grade. These articles offer endless speculation about the reasons why. Does the system favour applications from independent schools? Does it disadvantage those from state schools? What about those from inner cities? Is the whole system just a lottery? Does luck come into it? Well, logic tells us that if high numbers of applicants are going to choose the same universities or courses, more of them have to be unsuccessful, however careful the selection process.

This book doesn't tell you which college or university you should go to or which course you should do. That is an individual decision which only you can make – with the help of your teachers, tutors, careers advisers, family and friends.

So that is about what this book is not. What are its aims, then?

Quite simply, to help you as far as possible to find a place on a good course. As the title states, the book is to help you get into the UK's best universities and courses. These are not necessarily the same thing. Why's that?

- Universities are big places, offering a whole range of different courses. Some courses are bound to be better than others.
- Some universities have strong reputations in particular subjects or subject areas.
- Reputations change over time. A college or university which comes top of the tables one year may not do so well another year.
- Some of the best courses are not even in universities. Many of the creative and performing arts courses with the best reputations, for example, are in institutions which do not call themselves universities.
- Not all universities offer every subject area or course.

Above all – the best course at the best university is the one which suits you best. You will base your choice on a range of different factors, some of which are to do with the institution and some to do with the course. And other factors will come into your decision, such as distance from home, your interests outside the course, whether you want to work while you are studying and opportunities for study abroad or industrial placements.

WHAT DO WE MEAN BY BEST?

You can't do journalism at Bristol, physiotherapy at Cambridge, accountancy at Oxford or pharmacy at Sheffield – but these are all highly rated universities where you can apply to do lots of other courses.

Some universities have acquired higher status than others. How do you attempt to rate them? There are several 'league tables' – Chapter 3 discusses some of them. Each claims to be the definitive one. Some are based on measurable (quantitative) data, such as student to staff ratio or research funding, and others give more weight to less measurable (qualitative) factors, such as student satisfaction.

You've probably heard the quotation 'Lies, damned lies and statistics'. This is not to say that all statistics are lies, but it does mean that you can use statistics to prove almost anything you like. Even when statistics are valid and have been carefully collected and compiled, before you start to look at them you have to know what you are looking for and what they are measuring.

You might assume, for instance, that the best universities are the ones that attract the greatest number of applicants. Each year UCAS publishes the number of applications received by every university and college. For example, for 2009 entry, the 20 universities shown in Table 1 had the highest number of applications.

TABLE 1. APPLICATIONS TO UK HIGHER EDUCATION INSTITUTIONS IN 2009

University of Manchester	56,477
Manchester Metropolitan University	54,286
University of Leeds	52,823
The University of Nottingham	48,904
Sheffield Hallam University	46,218
The University of Edinburgh	45,868
Kingston University	44,083
The University of Birmingham	43,383
Leeds Metropolitan University	42,068
The University of Sheffield	39,920
Nottingham Trent University	39,525
University of Bristol	39,420
University of Southampton	38,410
King's College, London (University of London)	37,046
University of Brighton	36,870
The University of Warwick	34,868
University College, London (University of London)	34,559
Liverpool John Moores University	34,182
University of the West of England, Bristol	34,111
University of the Arts London	34,009

Reprinted with kind permission from UCAS. www.ucas.co.uk

Let's look at the top of the table – The University of Manchester, Manchester Metropolitan University (MMU) and the University of Leeds. Manchester is, according to its website, 'Britain's largest single site university' (with over 37,000 students), so you would perhaps expect it to attract the greatest number of applications. Similarly, MMU has 34,000 students and Leeds has over 32,500.

Any surprises on the list? Most of the higher education institutions attracting the largest number of applications have had a long time to build their reputations. But there are some on the list that didn't even gain university status until 1992 – including MMU right there near the top, along with Sheffield Hallam, Kingston, Leeds Metropolitan and Liverpool John Moores, for example. Yet, in less than 20 years they are attracting as many applications as some of the UK's oldest institutions.

There are many factors involved in people's choice of university. If you are involved in making that choice at the moment you will know the factors there are to take into account. All these will affect the number of applications a university receives and a few of these are given below.

Geographical location will make a difference – whether a university is in or near a city or whether it is in a rural area. The list above also doesn't take into account the number or range of subjects and courses offered. It stands to reason that a specialist drama school is going to draw applicants from a very small pool – and you can bet your life that most of them will be talented, thus increasing the competition for places – compared with a large university offering almost every course possible.

The top 20 list in Table 1 includes applications from overseas. London and other major cities may be popular with international students, as they are perhaps more likely to have heard of them. Some universities attract a lot of local applicants who prefer not to leave their home areas. And the small numbers applying to Oxford and Cambridge are at least partly accounted for by the fact that there is some pre-selection – schools and colleges normally only recommend students to apply to either of these two universities if they have a strong chance of getting in.

So maybe numbers of applications isn't the best way to decide which are the best universities. Other ways to compile lists could be based on, for example, entry grades required (making the assumption that if these are high then the status of the university must also be so), employment rates of graduates, number of first-class honours degrees awarded, percentage of students who can be accommodated in halls of residence or the resources available to students.

Chapter 3 includes some of the most widely regarded and often-quoted league tables with details of which factors they use to rank universities.

You may also hear people talk about the Russell Group. What is this? It represents 20 leading UK universities. The name is taken from the London hotel where representatives of these universities first met to set up the group. Member universities pride themselves on their reputation for high standards in teaching, research and links with employers.

Their staff produce research which is highly rated in research assessment exercises. They sometimes speak as a group on matters such as entry requirements, entry standards and so on. The members are:

- University of Birmingham
- University of Bristol
- University of Cambridge
- Cardiff University
- University of Edinburgh
- University of Glasgow
- Imperial College, London
- King's College, London
- University of Leeds
- University of Liverpool
- London School of Economics and Political Science (LSE)
- University of Manchester
- Newcastle University
- University of Nottingham
- University of Oxford
- Queen's University Belfast
- University of Sheffield
- University of Southampton
- University College, London (UCL)
- University of Warwick.

Half a million students are enrolled at Russell Group universities – one in five of all higher education students in the UK.

For many people this is the 'A list'. They are often referred to in the media as the 'group of leading universities' and because of this they can ask for high entry grades and attract some very well-qualified applicants. But even some of the most demanding universities have lower requirements for some of their courses. It all depends on how many applications they receive.

How do we define the 'best courses'? Some people might equate 'best' with 'popular'. There is more competition for places on some courses than on others. If a course attracts a lot of applicants it will be more difficult to get a place. Selectors have to cut down the numbers somehow. They will expect high grades, often in specified subjects, along with good references. But just because a course is popular doesn't necessarily make it the best for you.

What it boils down to is that choosing a university or college is a very personal process. Different people are happy or unhappy at different places. You need to go to the one that offers the best course for your requirements, your personality and your future success. This book, then, is really about maximising your chances of getting in to the place you want to go to, where you will do the subject that you really want to do.

JOE STATHERS-TRACEY, HEAD OF THEATRE AND PERFORMANCE DESIGN AND THEATRE AND PERFORMANCE TECHNOLOGY AT LIVERPOOL INSTITUTE OF PERFORMING ARTS (LIPA)

'We have around 2,000 applicants for 32 places in performing arts and 1,000 for 28 dance places. The pressure is slightly less intense for technology and design – around seven applicants for each place. LIPA is not the right place for everyone. Some people may be happier in the drama department at a university which offers a more academic course. Our selection aims to find the students who will benefit most from the LIPA experience.'

As you start doing your research, you will find that there is a lot of information about higher education – much of it, of course, on the internet. Many of the sites offer advice on different parts of the application and admissions process. You may find the sheer volume of information overwhelming and a bit bewildering. In this book you will find, in one place, the information and advice to take you through the process. It draws together some tried and tested tips with up-to-date advice from admissions staff who are actively involved in selecting students for courses.

The book also includes the stories of students who have gone through the process very recently. You can share their experiences of applying for higher education.

One last point: some of the terminology in higher education might seem confusing. Royal College of Music? Royal Academy of Dramatic Art? King's College, London? Imperial College? How do you know which ones are universities? Well, the answer is that they all teach university-level courses (mainly degree courses). The difference in terminology is usually to do with the history of how they were founded (if this interests you, you can find it on their website). One way to avoid this sort of confusion is to use the term 'higher education institution' (HEI) which is what I have done throughout this book. You will often see this used when talking about places which offer higher education.

Possible further confusion might arise over how the universities refer to themselves – the University of Sheffield, but Lancaster University; and the University of Manchester, but Cardiff University. What's going on? Again, this is a matter of historical terminology and makes no difference to the status of the HEI in question.

If that's not bad enough, when you start looking at the subjects taught at HEIs, you will find that some are divided into faculties, some into schools and others into departments. Although they are not quite the same thing – they reflect the way each HEI chooses to organise itself – they do not have bearing on the status of a course. It is no better or worse to study business at a business school than in a faculty of business, for example. Similarly with medicine and dentistry – some places where you can study medicine are called medical or dental schools, others appear to be universities, while others still call themselves colleges. There really is no difference, as all undergraduate degree courses in medicine are at university level and are equally valid. So it really doesn't matter whether you choose to study at somewhere which calls itself a medical school – such as the Medical School, Edinburgh or Hull York Medical School – or a university faculty – such as the Faculty of Medicine, University of Bristol or the Faculty of Medicine, University of Sheffield.

CHAPTER ONE
WHY CHOOSE A HIGH-RANKING UNIVERSITY OR COURSE?

If an HEI's status matters to you, you will probably want to look at Chapter 3, which talks about league tables. These rank HEIs in an attempt to show which are the 'best'. As we saw in the Introduction, different league tables use different criteria for their comparisons. Nevertheless, if you are interested in HEIs' general overall reputation you will find that the same eight or ten names crop up in all the tables, however the table is compiled.

When it comes to comparing HEIs by subject a different picture can emerge. For example, in the *Guardian*'s 2011 subject tables:

- Staffordshire University was ranked third for nursing studies
- the University of Essex Department of Philosophy was ranked fourth (after Oxford, UCL and Cambridge)
- business and management at the University of Sunderland was ranked 14th.

None of these is a Russell Group university.

Some HEIs lead on more than one subject. According to *The Times* 2011 subject tables:

- Loughborough University was top for sports science as well as building and librarianship
- the University of Warwick is top in the American studies, communication and media studies, drama, dance and cinematics (film studies) subject areas
- the University of Nottingham leads the table for agriculture (joint first with Reading) and for pharmacy.

The rankings can change from year to year. For example:

- philosophy at Essex had moved from 22nd place the previous year
- business at Sunderland had been 95th
- the Department of Chemistry at the University of Southampton moved from ninth in 2010 to first in 2011
- the University of York was ranked top for nursing (taking over from the University of Edinburgh).

If you are going to put your efforts into finding out about well-respected HEIs and/or courses, you need to ask yourself first – what do you mean by a high-ranking HEI? Is it one at which you will receive good teaching? (See Chapter 3 again). Or do you mean one which is likely to help you get a good job?

EMPLOYERS

Does it really matter whether or not you graduate from a high-status HEI? It can do, if you want to work for a top law firm, blue chip company or financial institution such as an investment bank or major insurance company. Some employers recruit from their list of preferred universities. Employers' own websites often have information about what they look for in graduates in terms of degree subjects, class of degree and sometimes even UCAS points. (Yes, these can still matter after you graduate!)

If you already have some career plans and you know of some employers you would like to work for, you can go directly to their websites, and look at the 'Graduate Recruitment' or 'Careers' pages. Some give indicators about which universities they recruit from. For example, if you visit the Rolls–Royce website you will find that the company attends careers fairs or gives presentations at the following universities:

- Aston
- Bath
- Birmingham
- Bristol
- Brunel
- Cambridge
- Cardiff
- Durham
- Imperial
- Lancaster
- Leeds
- LSE
- Loughborough
- Manchester
- Nottingham
- Oxford

- Robert Gordon
- Sheffield
- Southampton
- Strathclyde
- Warwick
- York.

This does not mean that Rolls–Royce will not recruit graduates from other HEIs, but it does suggest that the company has found suitable applicants in the past from those listed and is keen to maintain contact. This is as much to do with the subjects offered at these HEIs (engineering, for example) as any other factors.

Many employers, though, are more interested in universities' reputations in a particular subject. This particularly true in vocational subjects or subject areas.

EMPLOYABILITY

Employability has become a big selling point for universities and courses. Most university academic departments include information about the employment prospects of those who graduate with the various degrees they offer. So you may consider this an important factor in choosing the best course at the best university for you.

Each year, statistics are collected which show how many graduates are still unemployed six months after graduating. Here are some figures for those who graduated in 2010. Consider the following, for example:

- overall, 8.9% were unemployed six months later, compared with 7.9% of 2009 graduates
- graduates in geography (7.4%) and psychology (8.3%) had lower than average rates of unemployment
- perhaps surprisingly, 16.3% of 2009 computing and IT graduates and 12.5% of accountancy graduates were unemployed
- less surprisingly, 6.2% of law graduates and 9% of performing arts graduates were unemployed
- graduates in medicine and dentistry are less likely to be unemployed or employed in non-graduate level jobs than most other graduates.

HECSU HE Careers Service Unit stats, 2010

However, these averages are compiled from surveys of graduates from all HEIs and can mask contrasts. Looking at it the other way – that is, the numbers of graduates who weren't unemployed:

- nearly 97% of 2009 graduates from the University of Surrey entered employment or further study
- 96% of journalism graduates from City University were in jobs or further study within six months of graduating (2010 admissions leaflet).

Compare these with a national average of 91% graduate employment.

There is employability information on most university websites and often on departmental and faculty areas, too – most commonly listed as 'employability' or 'careers'. You might expect this for vocational courses, but it is becoming increasingly common for traditional 'pure' academic courses in the arts, sciences and humanities. Here are just a few examples:

- the University of Oxford points out that classics graduates 'have exceptional intellectual flexibility', valued by employers in the rapidly changing modern world
- the Department of English and Related Literature at the University of York says its graduates have developed 'communications skills and critical thinking', making them suitable for a 'wide range of careers' in the arts and elsewhere.

Most higher education courses now include some careers or employability content. Some HEIs have custom-built programmes, for example:

- the Liverpool John Moores University World of Work programme has improved the employability of over 3,000 students since it started
- the University of Chester runs the Graduate Head Start programme.

Some HEIs build employability into their selection process as well, as we can see in the following information from LIPA.

NICK PHILLIPS, HEAD OF ACTING AND COMMUNITY DRAMA, LIPA

'We are always conscious of the employability aspects of the course. We see this as a vocational course - even though we do have students who may study for leisure or interest, or those who choose not to take up a theatrical career. We feel this is right if we are training people for what is a very competitive field. So our selection is based on employability criteria, i.e. who is likely to be able to make a living in the arts world. This means we are looking for candidates who are flexible *and adaptable and display drive, determination and commitment. We try to instil a work ethic, which is what is needed in the theatrical world.'*

As well as the university websites, you can find employability information on job-related websites such as www.prospects.ac.uk, which publishes an annual report called *What Do Graduates Do?*

There is career and employability information on the UCAS website. Some is linked to particular subject areas rather than individual HEIs, so it can tell you, for example, that a graduate in biomedical science will typically have the ability to 'execute independent research centred on data generation' or describe the knowledge, intellectual skills, subject-specific skills and transferable skills you can gain from a degree in hospitality. What these subject profiles will not give you is information about the employability of graduates of a particular course or department.

You can also get, or ask for, information regarding employment from HEIs themselves. Many include it on their websites or in their prospectuses. If it is not there, you can ask for the information. Recent destination lists are what you want. It may be published in different forms. LIPA, for example, produces an annual graduate newsletter *See Me Now*, which, as well as attracting prospective students, also motivates current students in the notoriously difficult employment areas of performing arts and arts management.

Statistics about what graduates are doing are based on surveys carried out by the careers services of the HEIs, who are required to contact students six months after they graduate. However, you need to be aware of the drawbacks. Firstly, like many surveys, response rates are not always good. Students (like so many other people) tend to bin postal questionnaires from former HEIs or forget about them, and contact by email or phone may not be possible. Secondly, it could be said that finding out what former students are up to six months after graduation is far too early. Many are still in temporary jobs at that point – or are travelling.

PROFESSIONAL RECOGNITION

The entry requirements for your chosen occupation or profession may influence your choice of HEI. These entry requirements often include an approved degree (or degree-level study). Sometimes the term used is 'recognised' or 'accredited'.

For example, if you want to enter the legal profession and become a barrister (an advocate in Scotland) or solicitor you will need to undertake further professional training – whether your first degree is in law or another subject. You may decide to take a law degree to reduce your postgraduate training – in terms of time and expense. But the law degree must be what is known as a qualifying law degree, which means that the Law Society (for England and Wales) has approved the content of the degree and agreed that it covers what is needed to progress to the next stage of training. The HEI website or prospectus will indicate whether or not the course you are considering is a qualifying degree.

Similarly, if you are planning to become an engineer and want to progress to chartered engineer status, you may want to check the Engineering Council website to make sure before you apply that your chosen course is accredited.

The same is true for all the health professions. The Health Professions Council has compiled a list of all the courses which are approved for the main health professions such as clinical scientists, physiotherapists, paramedics, radiographers and so on. Again, it is worth checking that your course is approved if you are intending to go on and complete the training for one of these professions.

It is particularly important to check whether or not your course is approved if you are thinking of applying for joint honours or any other course which combines two or more subjects. Confirm that it will still lead to professional qualification if that is important to you.

Also check carefully if the course you are considering has 'studies' in the title – engineering studies, law studies, legal studies and so on. While many of these are subjects in their own right, they may not be on the list of courses approved by the professional bodies and therefore not lead so directly to professional registration – or to the top jobs!

On the other hand, though, some combined honours courses give the best of both worlds – engineering courses combined with a language or with management will definitely give you the edge over other graduates. Some degree courses are four years long because of this extra course content, such as law degrees with a European language, where the third year is spent studying overseas.

Recognition is likely to depend on the course content. In some cases, the modules which you choose to study can determine whether or not the final degree meets the professional standards. For example, at Aberystwyth University, you can combine law with a range of subjects, including maths, politics or economics, by studying two-thirds law and one-third from the other subject. As long as you take the right law modules, the degree will satisfy the Law Society's requirements for a qualifying degree.

Just be sure that you research whether the course you are applying for fits in with your career ambitions. I have only given a few examples here. Most professions and occupations have at least one professional body to advise and regulate practitioners.

Some degree courses, such as accountancy, allow part qualification before you graduate. The University of Brighton's degree in accounting studies, for example, includes preparation for professional exams which students can choose to take if they wish. If you know that you want to follow a particular career, this may be an important consideration for you.

CHAPTER TWO
PLANNING YOUR APPLICATION

ost applications for higher education courses are managed by UCAS, the Universities and Colleges Admissions Service.

UCAS handles applications to degree, Foundation degree and higher diploma courses, including Nursing Diplomas. There are some exceptions:

- practice-based music courses at colleges and conservatoires: applications are handled centrally through CUKAS (the Conservatoires UK Admissions Service). There is more on this later in this chapter
- independent dance and drama colleges (i.e. those which are not part of a university). Each has its own application process and separate application forms
- art Foundation courses, or, as they are officially known, Level 3 Diplomas in Foundation Studies (Art & Design). Here, again, you will need individual application forms.

UCAS

UCAS is based in Cheltenham and acts on behalf of its member HEIs all over the UK. The HEIs pay a fee to UCAS to handle the applications. UCAS acts as the go-between, relaying the HEIs' decisions to you and yours back to the universities and colleges. You deal with UCAS from the time you apply for a course until you are enrolled on it. Once you are enrolled, the admissions staff at the university will deal directly with you.

UCAS also helps you, or your advisers, with any problem or questions – but only about the applications procedure. If you have any queries about the university or about the course, you direct these to the HEI itself. UCAS staff do not make any decisions about your application – whether to offer you a place or which grades, or points, you need. All admissions decisions are made by the admissions staff at the HEI you are applying to.

You may make only one application in any annual application round. The system is designed to detect fraud, such as people trying to apply more than once. This could result in an application being cancelled.

For most subjects, you can apply for up to five courses at the same time in any one annual round. There are some important exceptions:

- you may only apply to four courses in any one of medicine, dentistry and veterinary medicine/veterinary science
- you may only apply to either Oxford or Cambridge (not both)
- you may be eligible to make additional choices through Extra – more on this in Chapter 8.

When do you apply?

The UCAS system is huge – half a million people making over two million applications, with several universities receiving well over 30,000 applications and some over 50,000. A system this size takes time. You make UCAS applications up to a year before the course is due to start. So if you are reading this book after September, the application process for next year is well under way. Most higher education courses start in the autumn. Some, however, start later in the academic year than this – in January, February, March, April or May.

While Table 2 shows the schedule for applications for courses starting in 2011, the timings are usually the same each year. Those shown here are the final dates set by UCAS. Your own school or college may specify earlier dates to allow time for applications to be processed and submitted.

You should regard these dates as *deadlines*. The admissions staff at the HEIs are busy. Your application has the same importance as anyone else's but is not more important than the hundreds or thousands of others that each university or college receives. If you do not meet the deadlines, the HEIs do not have to consider late applications.

The UCAS dates are the latest dates for applications. Many school and college advisers suggest that students apply as soon as possible, rather than as late as possible.

TABLE 2. UCAS APPLICATION TIMETABLE

DATE	WHAT HAPPENS	WHAT YOU NEED TO DO
Mid-September	UCAS forms accepted from now.	Apply as soon as you are ready. The earlier the better – admissions tutors start to make offers as they read application forms. They do not wait until the closing date. BUT: don't hurry and cut corners. Take time to choose courses carefully and write a good Personal Statement.
15 October	Closing date for application for medicine, dentistry, veterinary medicine/science, and for any course at Oxford or Cambridge (including the Ruskin School of Drawing and Fine Art – the Fine Art Department at Oxford University).	Make sure the person who will be writing your reference knows that you need to meet this deadline and give your form to him or her in plenty of time. They will be under pressure at this time of year, with numerous references to write.
15 January	Closing date for all courses except those with a 15 October deadline and art and design courses with a 24 March deadline. (However, if you are applying from outside the EU you have until 30 June before you are classed as a late applicant – with the exception of the courses with the 15 October deadline).	Make sure your application is received by this date. After this date, your application will be regarded as late and HEIs will not be obliged to consider you.

(continued)

TABLE 2. UCAS APPLICATION TIMETABLE *(continued)*

DATE	WHAT HAPPENS	WHAT YOU NEED TO DO
25 February	If you are not holding any offers, you may be eligible for Extra and can start making additional choices.	Ask advice at school or college as to whether you should accept any offer received under this scheme or wait for Clearing.
24 March	Deadline for applications for art and design courses other than those with a 15 January deadline.	Make sure your application is received by this date. After this date, your application will be regarded as late and HEIs will not be obliged to consider you.
31 March	If you applied by 15 January, HEIs should aim to have made their decisions about offering you a place.	Consider carefully each offer before accepting or rejecting it.
6 May	If you applied by 15 January, you should receive all the decisions from HEIs by now.	You may accept one offer as a Firm Acceptance and one as an Insurance Acceptance. Think carefully, then reply to UCAS. NOTE: Some people may have had all five decisions before this date and will have replied already.
7 June	This is the last date to reply to any HEI offers received by 6 May.	Consider carefully each offer before accepting or rejecting it. If you don't reply, UCAS will decline the offers on your behalf.
30 June	Final date for late applications to HEIs. Any applications after this date go through Clearing. Final date for applications from outside the EU.	If this applies to you, find out about Clearing.
6 July	Last date to use Extra.	

19 July	Last date for HEI decisions on all applications received by 30 June.	Consider carefully, but remember you only have a week to reply to offers at this stage.
26 July	Last date to reply to offers made by 19 July.	Consider carefully each offer before accepting or rejecting it. If you don't reply, UCAS will decline the offers on your behalf.
4 August	Results are published in Scotland. Scottish Clearing opens.	
18 August	A level results day. Clearing opens. Adjustment registration opens.	
31 August	Adjustment closes.	

There is no reason not to apply early. There may be advantages in applying early – in some HEIs, admissions tutors offer places as they receive the applications rather than keeping them all until close to the deadline dates. Applying early may mean getting an early interview date. It is an uncertain time and getting some of the application process out of the way early in the academic year may suit you so you can concentrate on working for your exams. If you have offers to work towards, it may motivate you to study harder and get the top grades to ensure you get on to the course you want.

If you apply late, there may be no places left on the course(s) of your choice. Admissions staff are not allowed to offer too many places, so they may stop making offers once a maximum has been reached.

In deciding whether or not to apply early in the applications cycle, you may want to consider these points:

- however early you are with your application, you cannot have any influence over the HEI decision-making timetable. If you happen to have applied to an HEI which prefers to make offers later on, then you will just have to wait!

◗ it would be a pity to rush your application just to get it in early. It might be better to take a bit more time to look at and rework your Personal Statement to make sure you are happy with it before you submit it.

If you do find yourself making an application late in the day, for whatever reason – illness, delay by school or college staff, etc. – or if you only decide later in the application cycle that you want to apply for a higher education course, don't worry! It's still worth applying and there are still likely to be places left.

Early deadlines

Some courses have an early UCAS deadline of 15 October. These are:

◗ any course at Oxford or Cambridge (including the Ruskin School of Drawing and Fine Art – the fine art department at Oxford University).

Courses at any HEI in:

◗ medicine (A100, A101, A103, A104, A105, A106 and A300)
◗ dentistry (A200, A201, A202, A203, A204, A205, A206 and A400)
◗ veterinary medicine or veterinary science (D100 or D101).

Art and design courses

Some art and design courses have the same deadline as most applications (15 January). Others have a deadline of 24 March (but note the 15 October deadline for the Ruskin School of Drawing and Fine Art). This is to allow students taking a Diploma in Foundation Studies (Art & Design) course to put together a portfolio of work to present at interviews. You will need to check individual HEI websites for the courses you are interested in to see which date applies.

If you find that the art and design courses you want to apply for have different deadlines, you can submit your application by 15 January for courses with that deadline and add further choices before 24 March (as long as you haven't used all five choices).

Until 2010, there were two different ways to apply for art and design courses – Route A and Route B. This is no longer the case: all applications go through the same route as applications for other subjects and courses.

Additional tests

Some universities and some courses ask or recommend that you sit additional admissions tests. Some are standard tests which are used by many universities in particular subjects. Others tests are specific to particular universities. The tests are usually sat in November and December. It is very important to check the requirements of any course you are interested in applying for and the arrangements for any tests.

The main subjects which require tests are *law, medicine, dentistry* and *veterinary science*. Some universities (particularly Oxford and Cambridge) set their own tests in popular subjects such as history or English. Chapter 6 has more information about the tests – their content and the arrangements for taking them.

Some universities (again, mainly the Oxford and Cambridge colleges) ask you to submit pieces of work. More on this can be found in Chapter 6.

Oxford and Cambridge applications

All applicants to the University of Cambridge will be asked to complete a Supplementary Application Questionnaire (SAQ). The deadline for returning the SAQ is on the corresponding page of the university website – for 2010, it was 22 October. Applicants are usually expected to complete the SAQ online, unless there is a good reason why they cannot (such as a disability or no email address). The purpose of the SAQ is to collect information which is not on the UCAS form, such as details of the modules studied for AS and A levels.

The University of Oxford does not require a separate application form.

Please note that you cannot apply to both Cambridge and Oxford in the same year.

Additional application information

Other HEIs or departments, as well as Cambridge, may ask you for extra information, often in the form of an additional application form or questionnaire. Chapter 5 has more details and some examples.

HOW TO APPLY THROUGH UCAS

UCAS uses an online application system known as Apply (at www.ucas.com/students/apply). You can access Apply from any number of computers – so you can do different sections of the application at different times. Your application is stored by UCAS and will appear each time you log on. You will be able to change any of the information that you have entered until you are satisfied with it and are ready to submit it. You may want to begin or do some of it at your school or college, but you could equally well choose to do so at home or in a library or other online centre.

You log on using a buzzword given to you by your school or college (it is the same for all applicants from that centre). If you are an independent candidate – i.e. not at a school or college – you can get a buzzword from a careers advisory service or Connexions and use that organisation as your application centre. Alternatively you can obtain a buzzword direct from UCAS.

The first time you enter your buzzword you will be asked to choose a unique username and password which you need to enter each time. You will also be asked four security questions.

Technical requirements

You need to make sure that the computer you are using can meet all these technical specifications:

- Internet Explorer version 5 or higher or Mozilla Firefox version 2.0 or higher (Safari and Mozilla Firefox for Apple Mac users)
- JavaScript enabled
- 128-bit encryption enabled
- monitor size 15 inches or more
- display set to 256 colours minimum
- screen resolution of 800 x 600 or above
- browser configured to use HTTP/1.1.

Schools, colleges and careers or Connexions centres should have suitable computers. If you are using your home computer, you might need to check the manual.

You can choose to complete your application in either English or Welsh. There are online instructions for each section, and Apply also has Help sections on each page, which should help you with any points you are unsure of. If you cannot find the answers there you can contact the UCAS Customer Service Unit on 0871 468 0468.

UCAS application stages

The application contains the following sections:

- Registration
- Personal Details
- Additional Information (UK applicants only)
- Choices
- Education
- Employment
- Personal Statement
- Reference
- Declaration
- Pay and Send.

Registration

In this first section, you are asked to give your name, address, gender, date of birth and contact details. The system then gives you your username and you choose your password. You will need these whenever you log on.

Personal Details

You will see some of these already completed, copied from the registration section you have completed. Now is the time to check that they are correct. Here you are asked for additional information such as nationality and any disabilities you may have. If you make a mistake here, Apply will note this and ask you to correct it.

Additional Information

This section is for UK applicants only and asks for more personal details such as ethnic origin. Some people see this as irrelevant; others see it as sensitive, but this information will not affect your chances of getting a place in any way.

It is intended to help UCAS and HEIs monitor equal opportunities. There is also a chance to enter up to two activities which you have undertaken in preparation for higher education, such as taster days or summer schools (but not open days). This section also allows you to add details about care and parental information.

Choices

This is where you list your chosen courses and HEIs. It does not matter which order you put them in as you are not expressing a preference. The system will put them into alphabetical order later. You do need, though, to give the HEIs' names and institution codes and the course code. Check carefully that you have used the right code. If you put the wrong code against a course title in any place, Apply will alert you. What the system cannot do, however, is tell you if you used the wrong code *and* the wrong course title. This is possible. Lots of applicants have been known to apply to the wrong HEI or to put, say, the code for one course when they meant a different one. In this section you must also state whether you are applying for deferred entry (i.e. you are applying now but want to take up the place a year later).

Education

Here, you give the schools or colleges you have attended and all the relevant qualifications you have achieved plus the ones you are taking.

Employment

In this section, you put the details of up to five *paid* jobs you have had, including employers' names and addresses, a description of the work and relevant dates. Details of unpaid work can be included in your Personal Statement.

Personal Statement

This statement tells your chosen HEIs why you are applying for the courses you have chosen and what makes you a good applicant. It is the only section of the application that wants something other than facts from you – it gives you the chance to show your enthusiasm and commitment and what makes you unique. See Chapter 5 for advice on how to complete this part of the application.

Reference

Your application must contain a reference from someone who is able to write about you and your suitability for the course. The usual people to ask are personal tutors, form teachers, heads of year or careers advisers. If you are at a school or college, whoever is in charge of the UCAS applications will tell you who to ask. This section of the application will then be completed before it is sent to UCAS. If you are not applying through a school or college, you should first approach a potential referee such as an employer or former teacher, get their agreement to provide a reference and ask them to send it to you so that you can paste it into this section. Alternatively, you can enter their contact details into the Reference section and UCAS will send them an email providing them with a login.

Declaration

When you have filled in each section and marked it as complete you need to read the declaration and confirm that you agree to its terms. The terms include the UCAS rules on providing false or misleading information in order to gain a higher education place.

Pay and Send

There is a fee for UCAS applications – £21 (or £11 if you apply for only one course) for 2011 entry.

Your school or college will tell you how they want you to deal with this section. Many have an arrangement to make one payment to UCAS on behalf of all their applicants. Otherwise you can pay online, using a credit or debit card.

That's it. The application now goes to UCAS for processing.

After you apply

When UCAS receives your application the staff check that it is complete and that the courses you have applied for are still available. At this stage they also check that you have not already made an application in this cycle. UCAS will contact you if there are any queries.

They then send a copy to each of your chosen HEIs. If you have applied for more than one course at a particular HEI, UCAS sends a copy of your

TIPS

- Have all the information you will need – exam results, details of jobs and employers, dates of attendance at different schools if relevant, names of HEIs and course codes all ready and to hand before you start the first sections.

- Do give details of any jobs you have had – even holiday or weekend ones. Admissions staff like to know about these. There is more information on this in Chapters 4 and 5.

- Print off hard copies at different stages of the application and check them. It's easier to read through and revise text on paper.

- Don't use the 'save password' option. Yes, it would save you having to key your password in each time – BUT: anyone using the same computer will be able to access your application and change it!

- Don't give your password details to anyone. Write them down and keep them in a safe place.

- It is a good idea to name someone who can act on your behalf regarding your application in case you became ill or temporarily unable to respond to correspondence from UCAS during the application period. There is a space on the application for you to do so.

- Print off and keep a paper copy of the application so that you can have it in front of you if you need to contact either UCAS or an HEI about any points.

- Make sure you notify UCAS of any changes to your personal or contact details. UCAS will pass on any changes to your HEIs.

application for each choice. Each HEI you apply to will receive your details at the same time.

UCAS sends you an Applicant Welcome Guide and a Welcome Letter. The letter includes confirmation of the courses and HEIs you have applied to. If this is incorrect, you should contact UCAS at once to correct it. The Welcome Letter shows the username you used to apply (not your password, you keep that safe yourself). The letter also gives you a unique Personal ID which you will use to log on to the Track service.

Track allows you to check the progress of your application and your HEIs' decisions whenever you wish to do so. The service is available whenever you have access to the internet.

As well as using the Personal ID for Track, you will be asked for it if you contact UCAS and if you need to contact any of your HEIs. If it's too long for you to remember easily, make sure you know where it is written down. As you progress through the UCAS application process, you will find you use this number so frequently that you start to remember it.

CUKAS

The Conservatoires UK Admissions Service (CUKAS) is the admissions service for places on practice-based music courses at the following institutions or conservatoires:

- Birmingham Conservatoire
- Leeds College of Music
- Royal College of Music
- Royal Northern College of Music
- Royal Scottish Academy of Music and Drama
- Royal Welsh College of Music and Drama
- Trinity Laban Conservatoire of Music and Dance.

You may apply for up to six courses through CUKAS, and up to five courses via the UCAS system as well, making a total of 11 in all. However, when you have all your exam results and receive unconditional offers, you must decide between the two systems and withdraw your application from the other one.

CUKAS is administered by UCAS and your details will be held by UCAS. The online application process is very like the UCAS one – with its personal passwords and usernames. As with UCAS, there is also a Track service and the option of using Extra.

You will not, however, have the option of making the application in Welsh. If you give the Royal Welsh College of Music and Drama as one of your choices and you would like them to write to you in Welsh, you may do this. CUKAS, however, will only correspond with you in English.

Application dates and deadlines

The CUKAS deadlines are different from UCAS dates – they are much earlier in the year. Table 3 offers the full CUKAS schedule. The dates are for 2011 applications, but are much the same each year.

Applications received after midnight (UK time) on 1 October are regarded as 'late' and will only be considered if conservatoires still have places left. From 1 February, applicants must contact conservatoires themselves before applying, to see if there are any places remaining.

TABLE 3. CUKAS APPLICATION TIMETABLE

DATE	WHAT HAPPENS
7 July	Opening date for applications.
1 October	Closing date for 'on time' applications.
2 October	Opening date for 'late' applications.
15 October	Auditions begin.
31 January	Applicants must reply to offers if CUKAS received decisions for all their choices by 5 January.
31 March	Applicants must reply to offers if CUKAS received decisions for all their choices by 5 March.
30 July	Applicants must reply to offers if CUKAS received decisions for all their choices by 15 July.
4 August	Publication of results in Scotland.
18 August	A level results day.
25 August	Applicants must reply to offers if CUKAS received decisions for all their choices by 9 August.
31 August	Final day for 'late' applications to CUKAS.
30 September	Applicants must reply to offers if CUKAS received decisions for all the choices after 9 August.

You will be notified of auditions and offers of places by email. Note that CUKAS charges a £15 application fee regardless of the number of choices you make.

CUKAS application stages

Like UCAS, CUKAS applications are made online (at www.cukas.ac.uk/students/apply). You will need to complete the following sections:

- Registration
- Welcome
- Personal Details
- Further Details
- Choices
- Education
- Qualifications
- Personal Statement
- Referees.

Like UCAS applications, you can complete different sections at different times – and from different computers – provided you save each section as you go along.

There are Help notes at every point where you might need them, but if you have a problem you can contact the CUKAS Customer Service Unit on 0871 468 0470 between 08:30 and 18:00, Monday to Friday.

Registration

You enter your personal information and contact details and will be given a username. You then choose a password. You use the username and password each time you log in.

Welcome

This section gives you your Personal ID.

Personal Details

Some of this is filled in automatically with the information you gave in the Registration section. You also have the chance in this section to nominate someone to deal with your application on your behalf if you are likely to be away or unavailable at any time during the application process. This needs to be someone who can discuss your application with the conservatoires and make decisions on your behalf. If you decide to nominate someone, you will need to decide whether this should be a person at home – a parent, other relative or carer – or a member of staff at your school or college.

Further Details

This section asks for information such as your nationality and any special needs you may have.

Choices

You can make up to six choices, listing the conservatoire and course codes. If you are not sure what level of course to apply for, you should discuss this with the conservatoire itself. You are asked to specify a 'study type', depending on how many instruments you want to study. Then you have to choose a location for your audition(s) – the number of auditions may depend on how many instruments you choose to study.

Education

Here, you provide details of the schools or colleges you have attended and of junior academies you have attended at any of the conservatoires.

Qualifications

Those required are ones you already hold and ones you are working towards.

Personal Statement

This gives you the chance to stand out and sell yourself to the admissions staff. See Chapter 5 for advice on how to complete this part of the application.

Referees

CUKAS applications ask for two referees. One reference must be from someone who can comment on your academic ability, the other on your practical music skills and commitment to a career in music. Normally this would be your principal study teacher or head of music.

You need to send the reference form to your referees. You can do this by emailing the form (as a Word Document), by printing the document and sending it through the post, or handing it to the referee. You have to do this for *each* referee for *each* conservatoire you apply to, so that the referees can sign the forms – which means 12 forms if you are using all six choices. Full instructions are on the References page of the CUKAS website.

Application and audition fees

There is a single fee for CUKAS applications, regardless of whether you are making one choice or several – £15 for 2011 applications. Audition fees vary depending on the conservatoire and the arrangements for the audition. The conservatoires also differ as to when they collect the audition fee – at the time of application or later. Some will waive or reduce the audition fee in cases of hardship. You need to contact the conservatoires to find out their individual audition arrangements.

Remember that if, when you have all your exam results, you are offered confirmed places in both the UCAS and CUKAS systems you must choose one course only and withdraw from the other system.

Some highly regarded conservatoires, notably the Royal Academy of Music and the Guildhall School of Music, are outside the CUKAS system. You need to apply direct to any conservatoires not listed under CUKAS. Each has its own application process.

It is worth noting that competition to all the UK conservatoires is fierce, since they attract applicants from all over the world. This is particularly true in London.

CHAPTER THREE
CHOOSING YOUR COURSE AND INSTITUTION

Having established that going to university is the right choice for you, you are now thinking about what to study and where. Which comes first, the course or the place? And when you are making your choices, how do you find accurate information to help you compare different places? This was touched on in the Introduction and will be covered more fully later in this chapter.

PLACE OR SUBJECT?

Whether you start with the place or the subject may depend on how clear your career plans are at this stage. It's easy for some people. They have always wanted to be a vet or an actor or have a passion for literature or the environment. But a lot of people simply don't know how to choose a subject at first, let alone where to study.

You may find that if your subject is very specialised, there are only a few places which offer it. For example, if you wanted to study Korean language or culture you would need to go to the University of Sheffield or the School of Oriental and African Studies (SOAS) at the University of London. Other subjects are offered by a larger, but still limited number of HEIs. Veterinary courses are an example.

Other subjects are more likely to be offered in particular locations. Oceanography for example, as you might expect, is mainly studied at HEIs near the coast.

Some people decide 'I'm going to University X and that's the most important thing. It doesn't matter which subject I do.' This is fine if you have a good reason for the choice. It may be near home (or far from home!), in a particular part of the country – near the sea, or in a mountainous area, perhaps – or have particular facilities you want to use, for sport or for additional support for a disability.

Some even choose a university and then try to use tactics to be sure of getting in – by looking for the course with the lowest entry requirements. It can work, but not very often. It doesn't work for two reasons. First, you have to get past the admissions tutor who is looking for evidence of enthusiasm for a subject and commitment to studying it (more on this in Chapters 4, 5 and 7). Second, even if you manage to bluff your way in, you are going to be faced with studying this subject for three or four years. You have to like a subject much more than you do even for A level or Highers, where it is one of three or four subjects. At degree level, you will concentrate on one subject or area. It follows that the work will be much deeper and more intensive. Three or four years spent on a subject which doesn't really interest you? That's going to be hard, however much you want to go to a particular university. It could end up with you dropping out.

WHAT TO STUDY?

Choosing the right course is very important. It's also very difficult! You will have faced these kinds of choices on a smaller scale when you were choosing your subjects for Year 12 and 13 (or S5 and S6 in Scotland).

You'll probably start by choosing a subject area. Again, how you go about this may depend on how far on you are with your career plans. Does it matter if you haven't decided on a career yet? No. Many people go into higher education not really knowing what they want to do after their degree.

It's fine to keep your options open. Plenty of employers do not specify degree subjects when recruiting. This is true even in areas where you might expect a particular degree to be preferred. For example, top law firms do not expect applicants for their graduate programmes to have a law degree. In many cases, employers positively welcome degrees in different subjects, as they recognise that different subject areas train the mind in different ways (and possibly attract different personality types). If they take a mix of people they will get a wider range of skills and abilities within the organisation.

And similarly, graduates of a particular subject can end up in all walks of life. You might find, for example, an English graduate working as a web consultant, a philosophy graduate in publishing, a classics graduate in human resources, a modern languages graduate in management consultancy and a historian in investment banking.

However, if your career plans are starting to take shape and you do have some idea about where you want to go after your degree, it is worth doing your research now so that you can choose a degree course with that in mind.

One of the big decisions is whether to continue with a subject you are already doing or to go for a new subject. If you decide to take a new subject, this could still be related to one of your A level subjects. For example:

- if you enjoy biology, you may want to study environmental science, oceanography or forestry
- if you have studied a language, you might want to explore the culture surrounding it or take a degree in a language that is new to you
- if you have a flair for physics and maths you may want to study engineering.

The opportunity to try something different may be just what you want, but do check exactly what the subject involves before applying, or you may end up disappointed.

When you have chosen a subject you then have to decide how far you want to specialise. You have much more choice over the content of your degree than you do with school subjects. If you decide to stick with, say, your favourite A level subject, you will know which parts of your course you have particularly enjoyed.

But there will also be an opportunity to specialise in subjects that are new to you. If it's hard to decide how to specialise in a subject you are already familiar with, it'll be even harder in a new area! Don't despair, though. If you aren't certain yet, make sure you choose a general course in the subject. You will be able to pick options as you go along, in the second and third years. At this stage, the important thing is to look at the web pages of the academic department at the HEI to see what options (modules) they offer. If these match your interests, then this may be the course for you.

Take history courses, for example. Around 100 HEIs offer history as a single subject – a total of over 500 courses – with specialist courses including European, Welsh, business, church, maritime, political or even garden history. And that's before you've looked at courses which combine history with another subject such as a language, politics, economics or sociology.

It is indeed possible to combine many different subjects. A combined or joint course provides a good way to sample something new while sticking with a known subject. If you are having trouble deciding which subject to study, this may be an option for you, especially if you have a strong interest in more than one area. For example, you may wish to pursue an interest in business studies while learning Spanish. Do a search and you will easily find courses that combine the two, many of which offer Spanish at beginners' level. There are various ways of mixing and matching the subjects – equal study of both or a major/minor combination of subjects, which means you can devote more time to one of them.

'But is a two-subject degree as good a single one?' you might wonder. Combined and joint honours does mean that you can't generally study each subject to the same depth. If you were thinking of going on to further, postgraduate study with the aim of an academic career, then it would be better to study one subject to a greater depth. If you are thinking of doing a vocational subject, you also need to take into account whether the course content will still satisfy entry requirements for your future profession.

Some of these suggestions will immediately appeal and others will not, so you can see how your interests lead you in a certain direction. What you can be sure of, though, is that, with over 50,000 degree courses to choose from, you will find something which suits you!

WHICH DEGREE?

As you do your research into courses you will notice that departments are arranged differently at different HEIs, with a range of names. The subject(s) you are interested in may therefore be taught in different departments in different universities. Take the subject of English, for example. Table 4 shows a small (and random) selection of departments at different universities.

Furthermore, at Oxford and Cambridge, academic departments are called faculties – at Cambridge it is the Faculty of English and at Oxford it is the Faculty of English Language and Literature.

At first, you might find this confusing, but you will soon build up a picture. You might start to see how the department (and faculty) names can help you decide which HEI you want to apply to. If your interest is in creative writing, then Aberystwyth might be worth a look and, likewise, if you are interested

TABLE 4.   ENGLISH STUDY BY DEPARTMENT

English is taught in the Department of . . .	at . . .
English Literature and Creative Writing	Aberystwyth
English Language	Glasgow
English and World Languages	Kent
English and Related Literature	York
English Language and Literature	University College, London

in how English relates to other languages, then you could see what courses Kent offers.

Even within the same faculty you may be able to study for different qualifications in the same department – seemingly in the same subject. For example:

- in the Law Department at Aberystwyth University, you can study for an LLB or a BA in Law
- at the University of Birmingham, geography degrees are taught in the Department of Geography, Earth and Environmental Sciences. You can study for a BSc or a BA.

It is important to remember that they appear as separate courses for exactly that reason – they are different. You need to check out what those differences are to make sure you apply for the right course. It should be clear on the department's web pages. If it's not entirely clear, or you have further questions, contact the department.

Some subject areas offer courses at different levels. If you decide to study engineering, for example, as well as deciding which area of engineering suits you, you will see that many engineering departments offer a BEng or an MEng. You will also notice that MEng courses are longer than BEng. The MEng takes you through the first degree (the BEng) and straight on to another year of study at postgraduate level. Some HEIs list the two with the same course code and others as separate courses, with different codes.

Courses with work experience

Chapter 1 looked at the employability aspects of higher education. For most people, their aim when they graduate will be to get a job, sooner or later – even if you want to travel or study further, at some point you will need to work! If it is important to you to leave university with as much experience of the world of work as you possibly can, you will want to look at this aspect of any course you consider applying for.

Some vocational courses include time out on placements, gaining practical experience to complement your academic studies. These courses are often known as sandwich courses. They are not necessarily to do with food technology or catering! What the 'sandwich' refers to is the fact that work experience is sandwiched between periods of academic study. They are sometimes known as a 'thick' sandwich with a whole year out or a 'thin' sandwich with two or more shorter placements. Don't worry about missing out, as everyone on the course goes out on placement at the same time.

You may already be used to combining school or college work with placements if your studies include a 14–19 Diploma, BTEC, NVQ or other work-related course.

The pattern and length of time spent on placements can vary. Here are some examples.

- Four-year engineering courses where one year is spent in industry, typically the third year.
- Social work students have at least two different placements in professional settings, totalling 200 hours over a three-year course.
- Language students commonly spend the third year of their degree studying overseas.
- On a nursing degree, students spend around 50% of their time on practical clinical placements over the length of the course.

In some cases, you can choose whether to apply for a four-year course with a year out or a three-year course without. The placement does lengthen the course, but also allows you to obtain practical experience in the real world – a definite plus when you start to hunt for jobs towards the end of your course.

Many vocational departments have strong links with relevant industries. Tutors will arrange for practitioners to come in to give lectures and seminars and work on projects with students. Students from the courses will go on site visits.

SUMMARY: TYPES OF COURSE

Academic degree
Usually lasts three years full time, though it can be four – a course which includes a postgraduate element and some combined honours, for example.

Vocational degree
Some degrees, such as medicine, dentistry, architecture, last longer than the usual three-year degree as they include partial training for a particular job and often need to be followed by more professional training to obtain the full qualification.

Sandwich degree
Includes industrial experience so, again, courses are longer – usually four years. Examples include business studies, computing and engineering.

Foundation degree
A vocational course with work experience and strong links with employers. Normally two years and can be topped up to a full (honours) degree.

Higher National Diploma (HND)
Two years full time, but some longer sandwich courses are available. Like the Foundation degree, it is vocational, has strong links with employers and includes work experience.

This is a valuable way of getting an insight into the areas of work your course can lead to. It may even give you ideas about careers you didn't know existed. When researching courses, you may want to look at the links between the department and relevant employers and organisations.

WHERE TO STUDY?

You will want to give some thought to the type of HEI that would suit you. Do you want:

- a campus university?
- a city centre site?
- a small place?

- to be near the countryside?
- somewhere you can carry on with an existing interest or sport?
- a chance to see particular bands?
- somewhere with a good reputation?

This is where your research comes in. A lot of this information is on the HEI website, often along with information about the surrounding area. You need to decide which factors are important to you.

Home or away?

Time to be realistic. Some people see higher education as their first chance to get away from home. If you thinking of applying to HEIs away from home, ask yourself the following questions.

- Have I ever been away from home? (It's a big step the first time.)
- Did I enjoy it? (Maybe you were with your friends then – when you start higher education, you may know no-one at first.)
- How often will I want to go home? (You will need to budget for rail fares or petrol.)
- How are my practical skills such as cooking? (A lot of student accommodation is self-catering.)
- What is the HEI's accommodation like? Will it suit me? (You may have to share.)

Some students choose to live at home. This might be for a variety of reasons, including:

- it's cheaper
- there's closer family support
- to maintain a relationship, or a friendship group
- to stay in a job.

Most people use varying combinations of these factors when choosing where to apply.

NARROWING THE CHOICE

As we saw in Chapter 2, the UCAS website is where you apply for courses. It's also a good starting point for finding out about courses. Whether you are narrowing your choice by looking at subjects which interest you or by looking at HEIs first, the UCAS website is a good place to start, as its Course Search facility allows you to search by subject or by HEI. There are also general articles on higher education.

Each course on the site comes with an Entry Profile. Each HEI has been asked to list information about the course you are looking at, plus some information on the HEI itself. The profiles vary in length and content, as there is no standard format. You might find any or all of the following topics covered:

- what can this course offer you?
- what are the entry requirements?
- what does the programme cover?
- what are the special features of this programme?
- what study facilities are available?
- what do current and past students say about the programme?
- what flexibility is there with this programme?
- what are the career opportunities?
- do you have the following skills?
- would you like the opportunity to develop these skills?

There are often also sections on:

- the institution itself
- open days, tours and visits
- interviews – whether the department uses interviews as part of the selection procedure
- admission statistics
- tips on application
- fees, bursaries and financial support.

Entry Profiles have a link to the HEI website – either directly to the relevant academic department or to the main HEI site.

For more detailed research about a course or HEI, as well as an HEI's own website you can use the following resources.

- The HEI prospectus. This is the HEI's brochure. You can choose whether to look at it online or as a hard copy. You may find copies in your school or college careers library or in your local careers advisory service or Connexions centre. If you want your own copy, contact the HEI and they will send you one. Every HEI publishes a prospectus each year, so it is important to be sure that you are looking at the current issue, as courses and other details change.

- Teachers, tutors and careers advisers. They will know about higher education, either generally or about particular HEIs and departments. They may know other students who have applied or study there. They may have visited the HEI or studied there themselves.
- Family, friends and people you know who have studied at particular HEIs recently. 'Recently' is the key: you don't want out-of-date information. Try and talk to people who have been to, or are currently at, the HEIs that you are considering. This can give you a valuable insight into what the social life, accommodation, sporting facilities and teaching methods are really like. Check where past students of your school or college have gone and get in touch with them.
- Higher education fairs. Here, representatives from various HEIs set up stalls with information and people to answer questions. This is a good way to contact lots of HEIs in one place on one day.
- HEI open days. These are easily the best means of checking out an HEI and are good for getting a real feel of what a university or college is like. Don't forget to look at the local area as well – it could be your home for the next three or four years.

Points to check

- Accommodation: what arrangements are available for first-years? Are you guaranteed accommodation? What are university halls like? Do they provide meals? How much does it cost?
- Departmental facilities: are they up to date? Do they have the latest equipment? What teaching and assessment methods do they use?
- Other academic study facilities: what are the library and computing services like?
- Social and sporting facilities: what does the student union provide? Does the sports centre look good? What clubs and societies are there?
- General impressions of the site: does it look like a place where you could spend the next few years?

HOW SOME STUDENTS CHOSE THEIR COURSES

KATRINA IS STUDYING BIOLOGY AT OXFORD UNIVERSITY

'Originally, I was going to study medicine. I'd wanted to be a doctor since I was about 16. But I also wanted to keep my options open, so I decided to study biology instead. I may still do postgraduate medicine so I looked at where people had studied who went on to the postgraduate medicine courses. Oxford was always going to be on my list – that had also been an ambition from an early age. I looked at the Russell Group universities, but discounted those in London as I wanted to be away from home. I looked at the course statistics – numbers of applicants per place and student satisfaction.'

RACHEL IS STUDYING BIOMEDICAL SCIENCE AT LANCASTER UNIVERSITY

'My careers adviser at school helped me look into the best places for the subject. I was looking for the best departments for research and the best funded. I was attracted to Durham, but in the end it seemed too far from home. Another deciding factor for me was that many of the course books were written by staff from this department.'

ANNA IS STUDYING MEDICINE AT DURHAM UNIVERSITY

'When I decided on medicine I was faced with the fact that I had only a limited number of places to apply to because I hadn't chosen to do A level Chemistry. I decided to drop general studies and take AS Chemistry plus Science for Public Understanding in my second year along with my three A2 subjects. It was hard work but it was worth it. My college careers adviser helped me to choose medical schools that did not require A level Chemistry. I finally applied to Durham and Newcastle joint medical school, the University of East Anglia and Sheffield. You can apply to Newcastle and Durham as one application and leave the two universities to allocate you to one campus or apply to both separately. I applied to both.'

ADAM IS A FINAL-YEAR DRAMA STUDENT

'I made a shortlist of 10 drama courses, choosing ones that were members of the Conference of Drama Schools and vocational acting courses as opposed to academic degrees. I soon realised that I needed to limit the number of applications due to the time and money I would have to spend on audition fees and travelling to them. In the end I applied to three.'

USING LEAGUE TABLES

AMIR APPLIED TO CAMBRIDGE

'I wish we had just one set of league tables that use the criteria that we as students would like to use. Also, the present ones contradict each other so much! I found that the University of Portsmouth came second in one and in another it wasn't even in the top 50. And the positions change from year to year. I looked at library copies and then, on advice from teachers, went online to find the most up-to-date data. In a lot of cases it was different in different surveys!'

How do league tables work?

The HEIs themselves have a love–hate relationship with league tables. Each HEI would say it is unique, aiming to serve different sets of students, and that therefore the tables are not comparing like with like. HEIs claim to be against the idea of comparisons and league tables. This doesn't stop them using favourable results in their publicity though!

Whatever the HEIs think, many people like to make such comparisons when they are deciding where to study. Choosing where you will take higher education is a big step, so generally students, parents and advisers find it helpful to have some data on which to base those choices.

The tables use various sets of data, obtained from different sources and given different weightings, to place HEIs in rank order. The first thing that many students and parents – as well as teachers and careers advisers – ask is the very straightforward question 'Which are the best universities?' and they then look to the league tables which rank the HEIs. Unfortunately, there is no simple answer to the question, as there are different league tables, compiled in different ways showing different results. Nevertheless, league tables do contain some useful information as long as you know how they are compiled and what they can (and can't) show.

The league tables are produced for three newspapers. Each is unique. Although they use the same data, they take different parts of the statistics that are collected each year and use them in different ways. What you will notice, though, is that the top of each table looks roughly the same.

How are league tables drawn up?

The main sources of information about higher education are what is collected by various public organisations:

- the Higher Education Statistics Agency (HESA)
- the Higher Education Funding Council for England (HEFCE)
- the Research Assessment Exercise (RAE), which is conducted jointly by HEFCE, the Scottish Funding Council, the Higher Education Funding Council for Wales and the Department for Employment and Learning, Northern Ireland.

In addition there is an annual National Student Survey compiled by Ipsos MORI, an independent market research agency.

Newspapers base their tables on public data from these sources, but they use it in different ways. Nearly always they look at entry requirements, student to staff ratio and employment rates, but with a slightly different emphasis. All place a high value on student satisfaction.

There is another source of higher education data, called Unistats. Its data its compiled by HEFCE (on behalf of the Higher Education Funding Council for Wales, the Department for Employment and Learning Northern Ireland and the Scottish Funding Council) and is available on the public site http://unistats.direct. gov.uk. This means that it is not sponsored by or published in partnership with any newspaper or private company. UCAS provides a link to Unistats. It does not compile league tables in the same way as the other services do, but it does let you do your own searches and comparisons, based on your choice of criteria.

League tables are certainly contentious. Some of the criticisms of them include the unreliability of some data, the sampling methods, the different weightings given to the criteria used and the fact that smaller specialist HEIs often appear at a disadvantage. Some also make the point that there may be very little difference in the scores of HEIs clustered together in the top or middle rankings. You need to be aware that some HEIs prefer not to be included in league tables.

So it is important when you look at league table to ask your own questions. Take one of the league table criteria – student to staff ratio – for example.

What does that actually mean? Does it mean that every member of staff is actively involved in teaching students and that classes are therefore smaller? Or are some eminent staff members always travelling to present papers at conferences all over the world? Do many concentrate on teaching postgraduates? Or on their own research?

THE LEAGUE TABLES

Please note that *The Times* guide is dated 2010, while the *Guardian* tables and *The Complete University Guide* are dated 2011, although they are all using data from the same year.

All the tables include subject rankings. Each has a search function and allows you to compile your own tables as well.

The Times University Guide 2010

These tables use the following criteria:

- student satisfaction
- heads/peer assessment
- research quality
- A level/Higher points
- unemployment
- firsts/2:1s awarded
- student to staff ratio
- dropout rate.

The guide also includes:

- an analysis of student satisfaction
- head teacher ranking
- peer ranking
- world ranking
- information on undergraduates/postgraduates
- information on teaching staff
- information on applications/places
- clearing entry
- bursaries

- scholarships
- information for EU/overseas students
- information for mature students
- the number of state school applicants
- information on applications from the lowest social classes
- information on applications from low-participation areas
- accommodation.

The guide gives further details about how the information is used to compile the tables.

The Guardian University Guide 2011

The Guardian University Guide 2011 is based on students' own satisfaction ratings for their courses, taking into account how satisfied final year students say they are. It uses 22 measures, including how much institutions spend per student, the student to staff ratio, employment rates six months after graduating and what grades students have to achieve to be offered a place.

The tables are compiled by an independent consultancy firm called Intelligent Metrix.

The Complete University Guide

The Complete University Guide site, www.thecompleteuniversityguide.co.uk, is managed by Robinson Digital Publishing in collaboration with Mayfield University Consultants and the University of Sheffield. The criteria used are:

- research assessment
- entry standards
- student to staff ratio
- academic services spend
- facilities spend
- good honours degrees
- graduate prospects
- completion.

The Times Higher Education Supplement
World University Rankings

This is a listing of the top 200 universities in the world. Although these tables are aimed at graduates looking for research places and university staff looking for international jobs in their field, UK undergraduates do study at overseas HEIs and it can be interesting to see how our HEIs compare with others across the world.

The information is compiled by Thomson Reuters, using specially designed questionnaires that have been devised by leading figures in the sector from around the world (rather than data from public sources). As it is based on totally different data from the three sets of tables listed above, it may be best to look at it alone rather than trying to compare it with the other tables.

Rankings are based on 13 criteria in the following categories:

- teaching
- research
- citations (the influence of the research)
- industry income
- international mix.

The top 20 British universities according to different league tables

The Times University Guide 2010

TABLE 5.   *THE TIMES* TOP 20 UK UNIVERSITIES 2010. NUMBERS IN BRACKETS ARE TOTAL OVERALL SCORES

Position	University
1	Oxford (943)
2	Cambridge (941)
3	Imperial College, London (859)
4	UCL (849)
5	St Andrews (842)
6	Warwick (830)

7	Durham (823)
8	York (814)
9	LSE (813)
10	Bristol (803)
11	Bath (802)
12	Southampton (783)
13	King's College, London (782)
14	Nottingham (779)
15=	Edinburgh (777)
15=	Loughborough (777)
17	Exeter (776)
18	Sheffield (771)
19	Lancaster (770)
20=	Birmingham (764)
20=	Leicester (764)

Source: The Times/www.nisyndication.com

Looking at the total overall scores, although Oxford came top, Cambridge is only two points behind. There is then quite a big gap between these two and Imperial College in third place, which is in a cluster of similar scores over the next few places. Further down, there are only a handful of points between the last six HEIs.

The Guardian University Guide 2011

TABLE 6. THE *GUARDIAN* TOP 20 UK UNIVERSITIES 2011. NUMBERS IN BRACKETS ARE PREVIOUS YEAR'S RANKINGS

Position	University
1	Oxford (1)
2	Cambridge (2)
3	Warwick (4)
4	St Andrews (3)
5	UCL (6)
6	Lancaster (16)

GETTING INTO THE UK'S BEST UNIVERSITIES & COURSES

TABLE 6. THE *GUARDIAN* TOP 20 UK UNIVERSITIES 2011 *(continued)*

7	Imperial College, London (8)
8	London School of Economics (5)
9=	Loughborough (10)
9=	York (11)
11	SOAS (12)
12	Leicester (15)
13	Bath (9)
14	Exeter (13)
15=	Edinburgh (7)
15=	Sussex (18)
17	Durham (14)
18	Southampton (22)
19	UEA (35)
20	Surrey (27)

Author: Jessica Shepherd, copyright Guardian News & Media Ltd 2010

The Complete University Guide 2011

TABLE 7. *THE COMPLETE UNIVERSITY GUIDE* TOP 20 UNIVERSITIES 2011

1	Oxford
2	Cambridge
3	Imperial College, London
4	Durham
5	LSE
6	St Andrews
7	Warwick
8	Lancaster
9	UCL
10	York
11	Edinburgh
12	Bath
13	King's College, London

44

4	Southampton
5	SOAS
6	Bristol
7	Aston
8	Nottingham
9	Sussex
0	Buckingham

Source: The Times/www.nisyndication.com

The Times Higher Education Supplement World University Rankings

TABLE 8. *THE TIMES HIGHER EDUCATION SUPPLEMENT* WORLD UNIVERSITY RANKINGS TOP 20 UK UNIVERSITIES. THE OVERALL WORLD RANKING IS IN BRACKETS

	Cambridge (6=)
	Oxford (6=)
3	Imperial College, London (9)
4	UCL (22)
5	Edinburgh (40)
6	Bristol (68)
7	King's College, London (77)
8	Sussex (79)
9	York (81)
0	Durham (85)
1	LSE (86)
2	Manchester (87)
3	Royal Holloway, London (88)
4	Southampton (90)
5	St Andrews (103)
6	Queen Mary, University of London (120)
7	Lancaster (124)
8	Glasgow (128)
9	Sheffield (137)
0	Birmingham (145)

This list is extracted from the World University Rankings published in September 2010

TABLE 9.   *THE TIMES HIGHER EDUCATION SUPPLEMENT* WORLD UNIVERSITY RANKINGS 2010–11

1	Harvard, USA
2	California Institute of Technology, USA
3	Massachusetts Institute of Technology, USA
4	Stanford, USA
5	Princeton, USA
6=	Cambridge, UK
6=	Oxford, UK
8	California Berkeley, USA
9	Imperial College, London, UK
10	Yale, USA
11	California Los Angeles, USA
12	Chicago, USA
13	Johns Hopkins, USA
14	Cornell, USA
15=	Swiss Federal Institute of Technology, Switzerland
15=	Michigan, USA
17	Toronto, Canada
18	Columbia, USA
19	Pennsylvania, USA
20	Carnegie Mellon, USA

Source: www.timeshighereducation.co.uk/world-university-rankings

SUBJECT LEAGUE TABLES

You have now seen how easy it is to get different results for overall ranking of HEIs by using different league tables. The same applies to subject league tables. You can use all the league tables quoted to draw up lists rating different subjects. Most cover individual subjects, except *The Times Higher Education Supplement* World University Rankings, which groups subjects into broad areas of study.

Here's how some more students made their choices.

ALEX IS STUDYING TRANSPORTATION DESIGN AT NORTHUMBRIA UNIVERSITY

'I researched universities very carefully using advice from my teachers and my own evaluation of courses. I looked at university and departmental websites and I read prospectuses and course details. I liked the situation of the university and its facilities, but what really stood out for me was the fact there were such good links with employers. I reasoned that if they had such good links with companies like Lamborghini, Porsche, Maserati, VW and Jaguar I would be likely to get a good placement, forge my own links and eventually get a good job.'

RISHI, WHO APPLIED TO DO AERONAUTICAL ENGINEERING

'I began by looking at some of the league tables, using both university and subject tables. I made a list and started to discuss it with other people. I found my careers adviser the most helpful. She really was a major influence in my choice but I also talked to former students from my school who were currently studying at the places I was interested in. When I researched the individual universities' websites, I paid extra attention to what was offered in each course, not only by the university itself. My priorities lay not with the social aspects of the universities, but with their academic background.'

CHAPTER FOUR
MAXIMISING YOUR CHANCES

WHEN SHOULD YOU START THINKING ABOUT YOUR HIGHER EDUCATION APPLICATION?

A s early as you can! As outlined in Chapter 2, applications open from mid-September in the year before your course starts and some applications close in mid-October, with the main closing date in January. By the time you start Year 13 (or S6 in Scotland), you need to have a clear idea about which courses you are going to apply for. Those closing dates may seem a long way off but they can creep up on you and take you by surprise.

It pays to get your application in early. If you do, you are more likely to receive decisions from HEIs early and can then choose between them and spend the rest of the year concentrating on exams rather than application forms and interviews.

Being this well prepared means starting early. Year 12 (or S5) is a good time to be researching – and possibly visiting – HEIs. By then, you will have started on your AS, Highers or other courses, so you'll be getting a clearer idea of what you want to study. Year 11 (S4) is even better. This gives you time to do some of the other preparation you may need for HEI applications – portfolios, related work experience and so on.

WHAT SHOULD YOU BE DOING IN THE YEARS BEFORE TO MAXIMISE YOUR CHANCES OF GETTING ON TO A TOP COURSE?

Be informed

- Find out as much as possible about higher education courses and the HEIs that offer them.
- Read prospectuses and course leaflets.
- Visit HEI websites.

- Ask other people for information – advisers, teachers, friends and students from your school or college who are now in higher education.
- Make some visits.
- Use your school or college's resources.

If you are still in Year 11 in a school with no sixth form and want to start getting information and exploring your options, you could go to your local Connexions, Careers Service Northern Ireland, Careers Scotland or Careers Wales centre. You may also be able to visit the library in the nearest sixth form college or your local further education (FE) college.

Higher education fairs

Many schools and colleges take their students to a local higher education fair. They are held at different times of year so you need to keep an eye open for advertisements. If you are in Year 11 (S4) and would like to go to one you could go on your own, with a group of friends or with your parents. Fairs are held in exhibition halls, sometimes on a university campus. Representatives from different HEIs have stands, but it is important to remember that not all HEIs will necessarily be there – only those which choose to be (or pay the fee). There is usually a UCAS stand too, as well as other relevant organisations such as student finance organisations. Some fairs include presentations on topics such as application, finance and student life, with a chance to ask questions.

Open days

These are held at different times through the year. Some HEIs have more than one open day, as they realise that people are thinking about courses and universities at different times in the academic year. There is no 'right time' to go – some people find them useful in Year 11 (S4) and others prefer to wait until Year 12, or even the beginning of Year 13. Open days are when HEIs show off their facilities, equipment, accommodation and environment. Again, you can attend presentations, this time on general topics but also on specific subjects. There are often separate sessions on money matters.

LUCIE FOUND OPEN DAYS USEFUL WHEN SHE WAS APPLYING TO STUDY PSYCHOLOGY

'When you see the campus you get a gut feeling about the place. Only you know where you will be happy. One or two of my friends, for instance, were put off some places when they visited the accommodation and thought that the rooms were too small. I found that I based my opinions on some of the subject talks I attended. If they were interesting I was inspired to find out more about the course. If not, I was put off by the thought of having to attend dull lectures! Most of the open days had the same format – campus tours, presentations on individual subjects, visits to accommodation and some general talks on things like application procedures and finance. I particularly appreciated the opportunity to visit psychology departments and see the labs and other facilities. Most places have current students acting as guides and answering questions. Talking to them is really useful. You feel that you can ask questions that you would not ask the staff. I found that they gave very frank answers. For example, at one place I was told "There is not much night life here but we make the best of it." '

Sometimes visiting one particular HEI can make all the difference.

STEPHEN APPLIED TO STUDY ENVIRONMENTAL SCIENCE
'At Plymouth, the lecturer who did the subject talk was amazing. I have never seen anyone more passionate about his subject or so keen to get students involved in helping the environment. I learned that the course emphasised fieldwork and encouraged students to go out and do things rather than sit in lectures.'

Taster courses

Taster courses are a good way to find out whether a course or university department is right for you. They are also a good way to convince admissions tutors that you are a keen candidate for their course. Many HEIs offer tasters, which may be in the holidays or in term-time (either way you need permission to attend). They vary in length from half a day to several days and are usually for those in Year 12 (S5). Some are intended to show you what it would be like to study a familiar subject at degree level. Others give you a chance to look at a new subject. Simulations, presentations, discussions, group exercises normally feature, as does hands-on experience where possible. Some include the chance to talk to undergraduate students and professionals in particular careers.

There is often a cost involved in attending these courses. Some are run by commercial organisations and charge a fee. Others are provided by university departments and are free. Even if they do not charge a fee there is still the cost of travel to think about. If finding the money would be a problem you should ask whether your school or college can provide any financial assistance.

Some of the taster courses are very popular and have far more applicants than places. Some have entry requirements. For medicine taster courses at any part of the University of London, for example, you have to be studying relevant subjects, with high predicted grades (but it is happy to accept applications for those studying relevant vocational courses such as BTEC National Diplomas).

PUJA WAS INSPIRED BY A TASTER COURSE AT IMPERIAL COLLEGE, LONDON

'In Year 12 I became interested in engineering, but wasn't at all sure that it was what I wanted to study or choose as a career. So when I saw flyers at school about taster courses, I thought that would be ideal for me. I had to apply by saying why I wanted to go, giving my first, second and third choices - Imperial was my first choice.

'Over the five days we were introduced to different branches of engineering. We did different practical exercises - in electrical engineering we built a radio and in civil engineering we had to build a newspaper model of the London Eye. It was aerospace engineering which really caught my imagination. By the end of the week I knew that's what I wanted to study. The week was useful in other ways too. We stayed in university halls and two students looked after us. I chose London as it's close to home but there were others from all over the country. It was good socially, with trips out to the theatre.'

Be prepared

If you are going to apply for a course in art and design, for example, you will need to take a portfolio of work with you to interviews. Tutors like to see how students' work has developed over several years, so it is worth keeping some of your best GCSE (S grade) and AS (Higher) work aside for this. They also like to see work you have done in your own time that is not influenced by teachers and exam syllabuses. It is therefore a very good idea to start a collection of pieces with notes explaining what you were aiming for in each one. This, too, can be started in Year 11.

There is no rigid format for a portfolio but there are some guidelines. Admissions tutors want to see a broad variety of work – drawing, painting from observation, 3D work and, if possible, computer-generated work and photography. An expensive folder is not essential, but its presentation is important. Work should be put in a logical order, which may be chronological or thematic.

At an interview you may be expected to present your portfolio to one or two tutors and talk about it. You need your best work in it, and pieces that you are happy to talk about. You won't have any way of knowing which ones you might be asked about so you need to be sure you can talk about each piece that you include. If you start work on the portfolio in plenty of time, you will be well prepared with examples of your best work to choose from.

SARAH IS STUDYING GRAPHIC DESIGN AT LEEDS COLLEGE OF ART. BEFORE SHE APPLIED THERE SHE DID A FOUNDATION YEAR

'One of the big things about doing the Foundation is that I already had my results when I applied to universities. So my offers were unconditional and I knew where I stood straightaway. I found the Foundation year really useful – between September and Christmas we studied a whole range of art and design – including drawing, painting, printmaking, illustration, graphics and jewellery – through project design briefs. After Christmas we specialised. The course gave me the chance to put together a really strong portfolio which I felt confident talking about at interviews.'

LAURA IS STUDYING GRAPHIC DESIGN AT THE UNIVERSITY OF SALFORD. SHE WENT STRAIGHT FROM SCHOOL TO UNIVERSITY WITHOUT DOING THE FOUNDATION YEAR

'I knew I wanted to do graphic design, so I didn't feel I needed the Foundation course. I had enough work from my Product Design and Art AS levels in Year 12 for my portfolio. Some places I applied to wanted the Foundation, but Salford gave me the chance to go straight on to the degree course. I think it was because I was very focused about what I want to do.'

Work experience and shadowing

If you are going to apply for a vocational course you have to convince admissions staff of your knowledge of and suitability for a particular profession. This is where relevant work experience comes in. Some work-related experience can help you while you are making decisions about higher education. It can also be a way of demonstrating to admissions staff that you have thought carefully about your choice of course and are keen on the subject. For some subjects, admissions staff will expect you to have some work-related experience.

Many schools offer work experience in Years 10 or 11 (S3 and S4). For some this is a useful experience, for others less so. Some people manage to arrange work experience that is related to their career choice and therefore relevant to their choice of higher education course. For some career choices, though, work experience is not available and there may be issues with age. Some hospitals and GPs, for instance, require students to be over 16 before they will take them on. This can be a problem for some school students in Year 11 who may still be 15 when they are offered work experience at school.

If you can organise some more work experience in Year 12 this will be very helpful when you come to write your application (see Chapter 5 for examples of how some students were able to draw on their work experience in support of their applications).

Another option is a work shadowing placement. The difference between work shadowing and work experience is that with the latter, experience is hands on: you get the chance to do some relevant work or parts of projects. Shadowing means spending some time with a professional person, observing their work and asking questions. They should involve you where possible and take the time to explain what they are doing. Shadowing is an obvious choice for professions such as law and medicine. It wouldn't really be possible to involve students in performing surgery or in a court case but there could be opportunities to spend time with a surgeon or a barrister.

How can you arrange a placement?

There are several ways – arrangements differ. Your school or college may allocate work experience for the whole year group – or use a local organisation working on their behalf. Or they might provide you with names and addresses for you to contact. If you have a particular organisation in mind because it fits your career choice, then you can approach it yourself. It may be a good time to use your own contacts, too, through family, friends or anyone you know who works in the relevant field. Try friends and relatives, neighbours, your friends' parents and your parents' friends. It's worth chasing up any lead.

By doing this you will be developing skills that will be useful in your university and working life. And more importantly at the moment, if you find and arrange a work placement yourself, it will be a definite plus point for your Personal Statement and for interviews. There is a world of difference between 'I did a work placement at XYZ Ltd' and 'I arranged my work placement at XYZ by approaching a senior partner'. Seeing this on your application demonstrates your enthusiasm and your initiative.

DIVYA HAD TWO WORK PLACEMENTS IN YEAR 12

'My careers adviser helped me arrange the placements. At Costain (an international engineering and construction group), I spent time seeing how important IT support is to a company, learned how companies tender for business and shadowed a health and safety officer. Another work experience student and I were given a real project to evaluate and report on. At Halcrow (an international engineering consultancy), I shadowed engineers in the drainage and sewerage department and did some calculations and flow rates for them. I also accompanied engineers on visits. One was to negotiate with a farmer who thought that a new mains sewer line was going to be too near his buildings. I thought that it was really important to get some work experience - partly so that I was sure in my own mind that this was what I wanted to do and partly to convince universities that I had done my research.'

ANNA ARRANGED A VARIETY OF DIFFERENT PLACEMENTS

'I learned different things on each placement and gradually I realised that I wanted to be a doctor. I worked in a pharmacy for a week and enjoyed learning about the different drugs, but I realised that I wanted a career with patient contact. I would have liked to spend longer than a day in the GP surgery, but it was difficult for the practice as they had to contact every patient who was due in that day and get their permission to have me present. In my week's work experience on a hospital ward, I wasn't allowed to do very much because I hadn't been taught any basic nursing skills but I developed a role for myself, did whatever needed to be done that I was capable of and spent a lot of time talking to the patients. I was allowed to observe several procedures too. One was a heart scan. We had just started to study the heart in biology, so it tied in really well with my academic work, but I didn't know very much. When the doctor asked me how many valves there were I got the answer wrong! I got really good experience of work with people with Parkinson's and Alzheimer's through placement with the charity Mind.'

Voluntary work

This can add weight to an application, too. It shows that you are prepared to give up your free time to help others as well as improving your skills and gaining useful experience for a future career. The skills you gain from your voluntary work will depend on what sort of volunteering you are doing. It is possible to volunteer in a whole range of activities, so you should be able to find something you enjoy and which is relevant: perhaps at the local animal rescue (for veterinary science), with older people or young children (for social work, medicine or nursing) or on environmental projects (for environmental science).

Even if your voluntary work is not directly related to your choice of course or future career, you will be developing useful, transferable skills, such as the ability to communicate or work in a team, so it would be worth pointing this out in your application. Chapter 5 explores ways to do this.

JAMES REPRESENTED HIS SCHOOL AT COMMUNITY EVENTS

'I volunteered to be part of the arena party for the local agricultural show. It meant three days out of school, but I still had to catch up with lessons and keep on top of homework. The show was hard work, but good fun. We had to make up the jumps for the equestrian events and then replace parts which were knocked down during the competition rounds. I've not had much to do with horses so it was interesting and something different. On another weekend, I was chosen to take part in a memorial service at the cathedral - we helped show people to their seats. Some were very old and infirm as they had fought in the war. There were people there from around the world and I was very aware that I was representing the school.'

JON VOLUNTEERED OVER THE SUMMER

'I worked as a volunteer steward at festivals. It didn't really feel like volunteering as I got to see some of the best bands. But having volunteer stewards helps keep the festival prices down and it raises the profile of the charity which sponsors us - winners all round! In some ways it was like a job, as I had to work shifts on a rota. This meant turning up on time, but if the next team were late for the handover, we had to wait, as we couldn't leave the venue unstaffed. My customer service skills developed over the week and I had to be firm in dealing with people - many of them a lot older than me. I had to insist that people showed me their wristbands and we often had to turn people away from popular events. When it came to writing my Personal Statement, I felt I had things I could say which showed another side of me, away from the school context.'

Performing arts and theatre

If you are applying for a course in this area – where competition is particularly intense – you need as much experience as possible. This is likely to be amateur rather than professional – though any professional work you find is likely to help your application. So you could join a dramatic or operatic society, orchestra or choir. You will probably do all of these activities in school or college, but if you have the time, try to get some outside experience too. It is important to get as much experience as you can. Admissions staff will expect you to have performed before you audition.

For technical theatre (stage management, lighting, costume design and so on), you will be expected to take a portfolio of your previous work to interviews. So, like the performing arts students, you need to look for opportunities to be involved in productions, in school or college and elsewhere. Your portfolio may include sketches, models, photographs and designs. It will take time to build up a strong portfolio, so the sooner you start the better!

Taking a year off?

As we have seen, many people get the work experience they need while they are still at school or college – by volunteering at weekends, after school or in the holidays or on placements during the school or college term. Another way of getting the experience you need for your application is by taking a year off after you finish your school or college studies and before going to university – sometimes known as a gap year. There are many different ways you could spend this time – working, volunteering, travelling or studying, for example. Chapter 9 has more information about how you could use a year between school and university.

Reading round the subject

In arts and humanities subjects you will be expected to have shown an interest in your subject by doing extra reading. English literature is the most obvious example. Reading the set texts for your exams is not enough. You will be expected to read more widely – writers from the same period as well as earlier and later writers and poets. At an interview, you may be asked about your reading. Seeing plays and films by those writers or the 'film of the book' will help widen your perspective, too.

Even in subjects where this sort of extra reading is not relevant, admissions staff at interviews will expect you to take an interest in the wider aspects of your subject. There are professional and academic journals for all disciplines which will help you keep up to date with current research and practice in the field. A few examples are:

- *Science*
- *Nature*
- *British Medical Journal*
- *The Stage*
- *Financial Times*.

Some of these publications are printed, others are web-based and some are available in both formats. Some are available freely online, for others you need to subscribe. Your school or college library or local public library may have copies or be able to help you access what you need.

It is also important to keep up to date with what's happening in the world. Watching TV news is a good start, but quality newspapers provide more in-depth coverage and analysis. Again, your school, college or local library is likely to have copies if you don't have them at home. The quality press is also available online.

NICK PHILLIPS, HEAD OF ACTING AND COMMUNITY DRAMA AT LIPA

'Nowadays, most young people's experience of acting is through TV, rather than the theatre. It's important therefore to go and see live theatre performances so you can start to form a critique of actors and acting. It's only by seeing a variety of live performance styles that you will find out which work excites you. Your own personal experience of performing needs to be as wide as possible. Just being in school productions is unlikely to be enough. Try to become involved in youth theatre or amateur groups. We do recognise, though, that this isn't possible for everyone – it can be difficult in rural areas, for instance. There are other activities which involve performing. Think about jobs in retail or leisure – or any interaction with the public.'

Choice of A level subjects

One of the most important decisions you make as you go through your education is your choice of A levels or Highers. (Those of you doing an alternative qualification will have had to make similar decisions about subject choice as well as deciding to take the qualifications itself, see p. 60).

At this stage, you probably know where your talents and interests lie. If you know what course you want to study, you can choose the A levels which will get you there. If you are less clear about your career or higher education course, the choice of A levels can seem harder as you try to keep your options open. The University of Cambridge offers advice on keeping your options open for the study of either arts or sciences by suggesting subjects which are commonly required – particularly chemistry, English literature, history, languages, maths and physics. (This would be good advice for those thinking about any of the top universities.)

Over the years, there has been some discussion about which A level subjects are accepted by HEIs and whether certain subjects are 'banned' by top universities. The Russell Group, for example, refers to 'facilitating subjects' – maths and further maths, English, physics, biology, chemistry, geography, history and languages (both classical and modern) – suggesting that these are the most frequent subjects to be required specifically for course entry.

The admissions sections of HEI websites give detailed information about recommended and required A level subjects and combinations of subjects. Most HEIs would rather tell applicants about what they do need (rather than what they don't). The vast majority of the information covers in a positive way what the HEIs are looking for but in many cases there is some mention of less acceptable subjects.

General Studies and Critical Thinking A levels are the two subjects which are often mentioned specifically in admissions information. A level Critical Thinking has a mixed reception. Cambridge will only consider it as a fourth A level subject. LSE's Department of Philosophy, Logic and Scientific Method, for example, excludes the subject from offers but acknowledges that it can indicate a candidate's ability to reason and follow an argument. General Studies is the only A level subject which Oxford does not accept for admission. Likewise, UCL and Warwick exclude both subjects from offers and specify that either can only be a fourth subject.

HEI departments often suggest relevant A level subjects. (In all cases, of course, equivalent qualifications are acceptable and the information about subject choice is equally valid.) Oxford's general advice on A level subjects is that candidates should study subjects which enable them to demonstrate their academic abilities.

Some Oxford departments are more specific. For example:

- the Department of Experimental Psychology lists English language, English literature, maths, biology, chemistry, physics, languages, religious studies, psychology, geography and history as 'ideal' subjects
- the three A levels required for medical sciences must include two from physics, chemistry, biology and maths.

Cambridge offers general guidance on A level subject choice by advising:

- at least two, preferably three, from biology, chemistry, maths and physics for science courses
- English literature, history, languages and maths as good subjects for social science and arts courses.

Other HEIs offer guidance on subject choice. For example:

- most courses at LSE require two 'traditional academic' subjects. The Employment Relations and Organisational Behaviour Group specifies an essay-based subject, giving economics, English, psychology or history as examples
- UCL specifies that at least two A levels should be taken from the list of 'preferred' subjects on its website – and that any language offered must not be a candidate's first language
- Warwick's general guidance is to avoid subjects with too much overlap in their content (giving the example of economics and business studies), because admissions staff want to see the breadth of a candidate's knowledge. It also suggests that subjects with a high written assessed content are likely to be a better preparation for study.

Other qualifications

As mentioned above, A levels are not the only qualifications accepted for HEI entry. Most admission information for non-Scottish HEIs tends to be based around A levels, as these are the qualifications studied by the vast majority of applicants. All the advice about choice of subjects is still relevant for other

SUBJECT-CHOICE TIPS

- Plan ahead! Look at admission requirements as you choose your A levels.
- Be realistic. If an A in Chemistry A level is beyond you, look for a course which makes lower offers.
- Concentrate on academic subjects – chemistry, English literature, history, languages, maths and physics are useful subjects for keeping your options open.
- All HEIs will accept alternatives to A levels, including vocational qualifications.

qualifications. Scottish Highers, International Baccalaureate, 14–19 Advanced Diploma, Welsh Baccalaureate and the Extended Project (among others) are all acceptable as well as vocational courses, NVQs, National Diplomas and so on. It is important to read both the HEI's and the department's policy on these qualifications, or contact the department if you are unsure.

FINAL NOTE

It is important to remember that admissions requirements – in terms of both subjects and grades – are not just the admissions staff's way of selecting the highest-calibre academic candidates; they are also a way of ensuring that, as undergraduates, applicants will be able to cope with the course. If a course requires A or A* in Physics and Chemistry, for example, you will need that level of achievement to get through the course without struggling. Results aren't just about admissions.

However. . .

Maybe you're reading this book having already made your A level or other Year 12/13 (S5/S6) choices and now realise that they won't meet the entry requirements for a course you now have a burning desire to apply for. If you didn't study academic subjects in Year 12 and 13 (S5 and S6), for example, or if you did a mix of A levels but now want to study medicine – don't panic.

Foundation courses

All HEIs are committed to selecting the best candidates for their courses. But they recognise that some people may aspire to the best universities and courses without being able to meet the usual entry requirements. Each Russell Group university, for instance, has a 'Foundation course' for this exact purpose. Here are a few examples.

- Nottingham has science and engineering foundation years, a preliminary year in veterinary medicine and science and a certificate in health science (for medicine, pharmacy, etc.).
- Manchester has foundation years in medicine, dentistry, pharmacy, engineering and science.
- Bristol offers foundation years in medicine, dentistry and veterinary science and preliminary years in chemistry, physics and geology.

It will take an extra year – and a lot of hard work – but it's never too late!

CHAPTER FIVE

WHAT ARE THE ADMISSIONS TUTORS LOOKING FOR?

The top universities and courses know what they are looking for in their applicants – and given the number of applications they receive and the ratio of applicants to places, they can afford to insist on them. It is important to read carefully the information the university department presents on its website. This will give you the specifics for the courses you are applying for. But there are some general points which apply across the board.

ARE GOOD GRADES ENOUGH?

There is no doubt that good grades are extremely important. Many admissions tutors for the top courses look at predicted grades as the first way of deciding which applicants to offer places to. Many prefer to receive applications from students who are predicted to get top grades – As or A*s, Grade 1s and Distinctions (or equivalent) – as they know that these students will have no difficulty with the academic and theoretical parts of the course. The content of some courses is written for high-achieving students and anyone who cannot reach these grades may have difficulty with the course.

But even for the top universities, exam grades are not everything. Alongside good results, admissions staff are looking for other factors in their applicants. Some of these are personal qualities and some are to do with activities you have undertaken and experience you have gained. University staff are looking for people who will succeed on their courses. They are also concerned that you know what you are applying for and that you are making the right choice of subject and course. It is unfortunate for everyone if students drop out of courses – expensive and distressing for the student, disappointing for the staff and frustrating for the good candidates who failed to get places.

Admissions staff have learnt over the years how to select the candidates who are most likely to stay on their course and therefore enjoy it and do well. Your Personal Statement on your UCAS application is your chance to convince them.

WHAT ELSE DO YOU NEED?

There are some 'extras' which nearly all admissions staff are looking for and some which are specific to particular courses or subjects.

The most important factor which is mentioned time and time again is a real interest in the subject. Words like 'passion' or 'enthusiasm' keep cropping up. Tutors want someone with a burning desire to study their subject. Admissions staff for vocational courses often talk about 'commitment' and look for evidence of students' motivation for choosing their course.

JOE STATHERS-TRACEY, HEAD OF THEATRE AND PERFORMANCE DESIGN AND THEATRE AND PERFORMANCE TECHNOLOGY AT LIPA

'We are looking for a palpable enthusiasm for live performance.'

This enthusiasm may or may not go along with good grades. Some students can achieve top grades effortlessly, without being particularly interested in any subject. Yet others can be really keen on a subject without having the ability to achieve the top grades.

Often, though, good grades and interest in a subject do go together. So tutors look at enthusiasm and interest along with grades. A candidate brimming with enthusiasm may be more attractive than someone who is purely an academic high flyer. Admissions tutors may take a chance and make a slightly lower offer than usual.

However, there are other factors which are of interest to admissions staff and can make a real difference to your application. These factors are likely to vary from course to course and subject to subject. Admissions staff are interested in the whole person – and interested by interesting people. They want their undergraduates to be a mixed group with a range of interests. There is therefore no blueprint for 'What makes a good undergraduate?' or 'What will get me on this course?'

The fact is that people with the highest academic qualifications could be those with nothing else outstanding to recommend them. They could have no interests outside exam work. This is not particularly healthy and could mean that they have to spend all their available time on academic work in order to achieve. This is not a good predictor for degree-level work, when the depth and pressure of work increases. Such people could sink under the load.

As a student at an HEI you will be offered some of the best extra-curricular opportunities of your life – sports facilities, performing arts, politics and so on. You will have the chance to participate in or organise any or all of these activities. So admissions staff want to attract students who have a wide range of interests so they can continue to contribute to the life of the HEI.

Activities outside your school or college work not only demonstrate that you have wide interests, they also show that you are able to manage your time. Whatever you might hear about student life, it isn't three years spent in the bar! Neither is it necessarily three years spent in the library or over a computer screen. It needs to be balance of work and leisure – just like your life probably is now.

No doubt, you are probably already used to juggling conflicting demands on your time – you want to go out with your friends, but when's that coursework going to get done? You're needed for an important match but you work in a shop at weekends. How do you keep up your music practice when you need to revise for exams?

It's going to be the same in higher education. And if you're away from home, all without the day-to-day support of family – no reminder to take your sports kit into college or last-minute lift into school because you overslept – while getting used to having to cook your own meals, do your own washing and live with other people with different habits.

HEIs want to know that you are used to juggling your everyday life – and still getting good grades. The type of activities you are involved in is less important than being involved in *something*. So whether it's a weekend job, voluntary work, sports or a hobby, the admissions staff will be interested to hear about it. Even better if it has some bearing on, or relevance to, the course you are applying for.

The admissions staff who really do want to know about your out-of-school or college activities are those selecting students for vocational courses. They will want to see evidence of your personal suitability for their course. So:

- voluntary work can be used as evidence of interest in certain health or social care professions
- work experience in industry can be seen as an indication of interest in relevant careers
- sports can provide evidence of communication, teamwork or leadership skills

- even a weekend or holiday job that you are doing for the money is helping you develop useful, work-related skills such as reliability, punctuality and accepting responsibility.

It is also useful if you can write about something you have done over a period of time. So, if you have worked for the same employer or been in the same sports team, drama group or choir for two or more years this suggests that you are not someone who takes up new interests at the drop of a hat and gives them up just as quickly. Perseverance is something else that impresses and points to a student who will not give up easily or keep asking to change options. Even better if you have achieved some milestones, such as music exams, team captaincy or promotion at work – this speaks even more highly of your ability to use your time well. Admissions tutors will consider you an asset to their course and their HEI.

You have limited space for your Personal Statement so it will probably work best to concentrate on a few activities. Admissions staff will not be impressed if you simply list a large number of activities. They are looking for some sort of explanation or evaluation of, for example:

- how the activity links to the subject or course
- what you have learnt or gained from the activity.

Key words and phrases you might consider are:

- academic ability
- enthusiasm
- relevant knowledge or experience
- personal suitability
- time management.

There is more on writing your Personal Statement later in this chapter.

HOW DO ADMISSIONS STAFF FOR COMPETITIVE COURSES SELECT APPLICANTS?

By using the following criteria:

- known examination results – GCSE grades and possibly AS module grades. Not all schools and colleges reveal these but the person writing the reference should add a sentence explaining their predicted grades – teaching staff are expected to estimate the grades you will achieve in your final examinations

- academic reference – this has to be from someone who knows your work and can comment on your attitude to work and your suitability for higher-level study. It does not have to be from someone who teaches you. Schools and colleges have their own policies on who writes or contributes to the reference. For example, each subject teacher can write a paragraph to be incorporated into a reference written by the personal tutor. Chapter 2 covers how to organise a reference if you are applying as an individual (rather than through a school or college)
- Personal Statement – more on this later in this chapter
- interview – Chapter 7 looks at interviews in detail.

Different departments – even within the same HEI – use different criteria. They use a mix of the above methods. Some, for instance, do not interview students. Some do, but only in certain cases. Others use known exam results and predicted grades only and simply make offers to those who seem likely to meet their admissions criteria.

Here are some different views from admissions staff.

VANDA FENN, FACULTY ACADEMIC ADMISSIONS CO-ORDINATOR, SCHOOL OF HEALTH AND SOCIAL CARE, UNIVERSITY OF THE WEST OF ENGLAND, BRISTOL

'First I check that candidates have the required GCSE passes in English, maths and a science (or accepted alternatives) and predicted grades in the region of 240-280 UCAS points, to include a science subject at 80 points. We accept PE and social sciences such as psychology and sociology in this category as well as the laboratory-based science subjects.'

PROFESSOR FRED LOEBINGER, ADMISSIONS TUTOR, THE DEPARTMENT OF PHYSICS AND ASTRONOMY, UNIVERSITY OF MANCHESTER

'We make a quick assessment of the applicant's potential from their UCAS application. At this stage we are mainly looking for their potential for A* and A grades. We adjust our courses to cater for students of this ability level and anyone not meeting these grades might struggle. We also look at the Personal Statement, school reference and GCSE grades. The Personal Statement is particularly important in borderline cases. We invite over 700 students for interview'.

NICK PHILLIPS, HEAD OF ACTING AND COMMUNITY DRAMA, LIPA

'We have set the UCAS tariff at 180 points to encourage as wide as possible a range of applicants and in recognition of the fact that we are looking for more than academic ability. For acting courses, we ask applicants to submit a written review. This is to test critical ability - which is more important to us than the writing skills. We are looking for people who have the ability to process and articulate theatrical work.'

EILEEN THEIL, ADMISSIONS TUTOR, THE SCHOOL OF DENTISTRY, UNIVERSITY OF LIVERPOOL

'When I receive the UCAS applications, I screen them. Our shortlisting criteria are mainly academic. Everyone who meets the shortlisting criteria is offered an interview. As well as the academic criteria of potential A grades at A level along with seven As at GCSE, what we are looking for in Personal Statements is a strong commitment to dentistry. Anywhere we feel the commitment is lacking or not strong enough will be rejected. For example, we would not offer an interview to anyone applying for both medicine and dentistry. Likewise, applicants for the BSc in Dental Hygiene and Therapy would need to make it clear that they want a career in dental hygiene and see it as a profession in its own right. We are not interested in people who have applied in case they don't get in to do dentistry.'

KIERON SALMON, DIRECTOR OF ADMISSIONS, THE SCHOOL OF VETERINARY SCIENCE, UNIVERSITY OF LIVERPOOL

'We look at Personal Statements, but we don't use them as part of the selection. Our first screening is academic. Applicants need to be able to achieve at least 2 As and a B (with a B at AS level) to deal with the course. Grades at this level are an indicator of the ability to juggle demands on one's time. We also need people to have a thorough and realistic knowledge of the job, so we place great emphasis on relevant work experience.'

PAUL BAINES, HEAD OF THE SCHOOL OF ENGLISH, UNIVERSITY OF LIVERPOOL

'Our offers are made almost exclusively on the basis of the UCAS form. We read each form thoroughly. I always read the Personal Statement and the teacher's reference as well as looking at the subjects taken at GCSE. In the Personal Statement we are looking for people who come across well and have an ability to create a narrative about themselves and express themselves in an interesting way.

We are looking for people who are interesting as well as interested in the subject. I want to know about their wider reading, beyond A level set texts. I also want them to tell me about their expectations for the subject and what they plan to do with it. I am looking for a strong academic personality. That's more important to me than an all-rounder. How they relate to the subject is far more important to me than outside activities.'

Some departments ask applicants to complete an application form in addition to the UCAS application, such as the University of Cambridge Supplementary Application Questionnaire (SAQ) mentioned in Chapter 2.

Here are some other examples.

LIPA

'Applicants for several of our courses are asked to fill in the LIPA form which gives them a chance to say why they particularly want to study here. From these we select the best candidates for audition or interview.'

KIERON SALMON, DIRECTOR OF ADMISSIONS, THE SCHOOL OF VETERINARY SCIENCE, UNIVERSITY OF LIVERPOOL

'We send a work experience questionnaire to all candidates who meet our minimum academic requirements. The questionnaires are scored and ranked according to the amount and appropriateness of each applicant's work experience.'

VANDA FENN, FACULTY ACADEMIC ADMISSIONS CO-ORDINATOR, SCHOOL OF HEALTH AND SOCIAL CARE, UNIVERSITY OF THE WEST OF ENGLAND, BRISTOL

'Applicants that meet the criteria are then sent a biographical questionnaire, which takes 15-20 minutes to complete. This is the BARS questionnaire - Behaviourally Anchored Rating Scale, which works on the premise that past behaviours are indicators of future behaviour. On return, the questionnaires are scored by administrative assistants but I look again at the ones that are just below the acceptance score.'

HOW USEFUL IS WORK EXPERIENCE?

It can be very useful indeed. Chapter 4 gave some examples of how students were able to use their experiences to add value to their applications. There were also some suggestions as to how to arrange a placement.

But what if you can't?

It isn't always possible, and people such as doctors, vets and lawyers are often overwhelmed with requests from students. In addition, they have the problem of contacting patients or clients to ask if they will agree to have a student present. If you cannot get any experience in the profession you are hoping to enter there are alternatives. You could, for example, visit law courts and observe different kinds of trials. If you cannot arrange work experience in a hospital or with a GP you could try to observe what goes on at a typical surgery. Perhaps the practice nurse or the receptionist could allow you to spend time with them.

What admissions tutors are looking for is applicants with a real understanding of the profession they are aspiring to enter. They want to know that you have a clear idea of the highs and lows of the work, the good as well as the bad – in other words, that you know what you are letting yourself in for. They also want to know that you understand the issues of the work. They do not necessarily expect you to know about all the latest research but they would expect you to know about current changes in the NHS, for example, if you are applying for medicine or dentistry, or child protection if you are applying for social work.

So they are looking for some sort of relevant experience but, just as importantly, they want to see what you made of it.

- Did your weekend job at a residential home inflame your passion for a medical career?
- What was it about volunteering to walk rescue dogs that made you want to work with sick animals?
- How did your visit to the local Crown Court catch your imagination?

The point is that a successful application is as much about how you talk about the experience you had as about the experience yourself. So if you can only manage to shadow someone for a day or make a visit to a site, don't worry too much. Just make sure that you capture in your Personal Statement exactly what you got from that visit.

PROFESSOR FRED LOEBINGER, ADMISSIONS TUTOR, THE DEPARTMENT OF PHYSICS AND ASTRONOMY, UNIVERSITY OF MANCHESTER

'We don't look for relevant work experience as it's difficult to get in this field. But we are looking for a wide range of interests, not just academic. We like applicants who have been involved in sport, music or achievements such as the Duke of Edinburgh's Award. It is the involvement which is important, particularly in areas away from physics.'

VANDA FENN, FACULTY ACADEMIC ADMISSIONS CO-ORDINATOR, SCHOOL OF HEALTH AND SOCIAL CARE, UNIVERSITY OF THE WEST OF ENGLAND, BRISTOL

'We don't expect work experience. Applicants under 18 are not permitted to do it, so we don't ask for it from anyone, although older applicants may have done it and write about it. But I am looking for insight into the profession - having made the effort to find out about midwifery and the work of midwives. They could have read books on midwifery and professional journals, visited a midwifery department at a university open day or arranged to go to a local midwifery unit and talked to the staff there about their work. In other words they must have been proactive.'

YOUR PERSONAL STATEMENT

You will have realised by now that the Personal Statement is very, very important. For many admissions tutors it is an essential consideration. Even those who say that they give it relatively little importance often say that they look at it last, rather than not at all, or that they sometimes take it into account if they cannot make up their minds on a candidate's suitability.

What to include in the statement

If you apply to a department that does not normally conduct interviews, this could be your only chance to impress the admissions tutors. If the department does interviews, your Personal Statement could be one of the factors that gets you to an interview. So plan it carefully.

Admissions tutors need to see why you are interested in the courses that you have applied for and evidence of the attributes described at the beginning of the chapter. Before you write your statement, it is a good idea to make a list of all the relevant information you can think of and then ask other people who know you well if they can think of anything to add.

It is worth including the following points.

- What really interests you about this subject, including particular topics that inspire you to want to study it in more depth. Include details of what you have read about the subject that is not on your exam syllabus.

This can be difficult if you have applied for different courses. HEIs that you apply to will not know what your other choices are – but they will all see the Personal Statement.

- What you hope to get out of studying the subject. This is particularly important if you have chosen a vocational course.
- Why you have chosen a particular course. If all your choices offer the same plus point – perhaps a sandwich placement or the chance to study in another country for part of the course – then you can say so. But if only three of your five do so you can't get away with it.
- What career plans you have (if any) for when you complete your course. If you have none as yet, it doesn't matter. Tutors know that students change their minds as they progress through courses and often have very different ideas at the end of three or four years.
- If you are applying for deferred entry explain what you intend to do until the course starts.
- If you are applying for any sponsorships give details of those too.

In Chapter 4 you were able to see how some students explained their interest in a subject and also drew on various activities and experiences to boost their applications. They used positive sentences that stressed the enthusiasm and commitment tutors are looking for.

Here's how two students were able to use their work experience in their Personal Statements.

DIVYA, APPLYING FOR ENGINEERING

'While shadowing a Health and Safety Adviser I visited the various sites where Costain was working and was shown how seriously the company took health and safety and also how important an issue it has become in recent years. By visiting a member of the public concerned about the company's actions I also got the chance to see how significant communication is in this industry.'

SEAN, APPLYING FOR BUSINESS

'I was glad I was doing the Advanced Diploma when it came to my Personal Statement. There is so much practical work on the course, I had plenty to write about. Part of the course involved setting up a business. We had to arrange placements for ourselves, and while I was at the local newspaper, I had to write a report on teamwork in the organisation.'

Some examples from Personal Statements

Subject-related comments

❝ Professor PH Kenny's *Studying Law* has highlighted that not all aspects of law are as glamorous as criminal law and some can be very challenging, such as the law of evidence, but all are equally important. ❞

❝ To explore what a psychology degree might entail, I read Steven Pinker's *How the Mind Works,* which I found fascinating, as he takes you on a journey to answer questions such as "Does the parent–offspring conflict begin in the womb?" and "Why did the mass murder in Dunblane happen?" ❞

❝ Visiting my local County Court allowed me to observe the legal system in practice, including problems that occur, such as the defendant's failure to attend and how the process of justice is dispensed. ❞

❝ I am very keen on applying for architecture, as I feel that my A level courses give me the perfect grounding for study in this field and I am interested and stimulated by the architectural ideas and work that I have read about, discussed and seen. My Maths and Physics A level courses have given me an excellent basis for the technical parts of an architecture course. Part of my art course was a project featuring styles of buildings, including the Sacré-Coeur church, other decorative features from churches and the major new shopping precinct in my local city centre. ❞

❝ To broaden my understanding of other historical areas I have joined my school's History Club and the city's Historical Association, where I have particularly enjoyed talks on the Holocaust and the Polar Explorations of Captain Scott. **"**

" I enjoyed my work experience at an architect's firm. This placement was organised by my school. I have arranged some further work experience with a different firm for the Christmas holidays, and I will be discussing the construction process with a site manager. **"**

" I have an interest in many types of art and have visited galleries and exhibitions in London, Paris and New York. I particularly enjoyed writing my personal study of Andy Warhol. **"**

Wider, transferable skills

" I have completed the Duke of Edinburgh Silver Award. This allowed me to develop my leadership and team-building skills. Sport has always interested me as a way of relaxing from academic study. I have represented various teams in netball, hockey and tennis. **"**

" I have worked part time for three large retailers and at the local leisure centre, and developed my customer service skills. **"**

" I have further contributed to school life by being an active member of the School Council and Sixth Form Committee, which involves attending regular meetings and communicating with my peers. **"**

" During my gap year, I intend to take an industrial placement to apply the skills I have gained and also build upon the current knowledge I have. I feel that by taking this gap year I will gain relevant background knowledge that will act as an advantage to me while studying my course, and develop a sense of maturity and also passion towards my career. *

' I have completed the Millennium Volunteer Scheme, which included being a Young Leader at Brownies, and I have gained a Duke of Edinburgh's Award, which strengthened my teamwork and problem-solving skills. *

Advice from admissions tutors

FRED LOEBINGER, ADMISSIONS TUTOR, THE DEPARTMENT OF PHYSICS AND ASTRONOMY, UNIVERSITY OF MANCHESTER

'We want to know that you are keen and be sure that you will cope on the course. We use the Personal Statement as the basis of the interview, so you may be challenged on any part of it.'

LINDA WILSON, ADMISSIONS TUTOR FOR BIOMEDICAL SCIENCES, UNIVERSITY OF LEEDS

'Before applying make sure that you know what you will be studying. This sounds obvious but you may be surprised to know that some students who apply for pharmacology think this degree will enable them to dispense medicines in a pharmacy. So when you write your Personal Statement, make it obvious that you are aware of what the programme entails. When reading the Personal Statement of a student applying for pharmacology I am looking for evidence that the applicant knows what they are applying for. You should justify your choice with an explanation of why the pharmacology degree interests you and give some indication about where you think this may lead in terms of a career.

'Like all the degrees in biomedical sciences, pharmacology is a good grounding to apply, on graduation, for a place on a postgraduate medicine programme. If this is what you intend to do, include this in your Personal Statement, as this shows me that you have undertaken some preliminary research and have a commitment to pharmacology.'

MICHAEL SNAPE, ADMISSIONS TUTOR FOR HISTORY, UNIVERSITY OF BIRMINGHAM

'My advice to applicants is to make it genuinely your own statement. It needs to be what it says it is - personal. Plagiarism can be an issue. I don't necessarily mean that students buy the statements on offer on the internet, but some have obviously been intensively coached. The same words and phrases often crop up. You need to tell us why you want to study the course, expressing yourself freely and with independence of thought. Tell me how and why your interest in history extends beyond the A level syllabus. Tell me about a strong interest you have, if appropriate, in a period that is totally different from the one you are studying for exams. Other than this, I am not particularly interested in extra-curricular activities other than the fact that they show some balance of time between academic work and other things.'

JONATHAN HOGG, ADMISSIONS OFFICER, SCHOOL OF HISTORY, UNIVERSITY OF LIVERPOOL

'We do come across very polished Personal Statements, particularly amongst candidates from schools which are used to UCAS applications. Some are so polished that it's hard to tell anything at all about the candidate. Ironically, a more "raw" statement can give much more of an insight and be more of a pleasure to read.'

Structuring the statement

There are several different layouts you could use. One is a three-paragraph format, with one saying why you want to study the subject, a second saying what you enjoy about your present course and the third about yourself.

Another is to have a new paragraph for each point you mention, for example:

- subject interest
- reasons for course choice
- efforts to find out more about it
- career plans
- relevant activities and interests
- other activities and interests.

BUT there is no approach that is set in stone. And more importantly, there is no single winning formula or foolproof structure. It is your statement and it should be as you want to write it. Schools and colleges usually give advice on

TIPS

- Your Personal Statement may be so much a part of you by now that you really cannot see any way of changing it. A fresh eye can often spot a sentence that can be shortened or a more concise way of explaining something. Don't be afraid to ask for other people's comments and suggestions – but don't feel obliged to use their advice. It's up to you!

- When you've finished, it's worth asking someone else to look over it to see how it reads, check for spelling or typing errors, etc. Again, that fresh eye may see things that you don't notice.

structure but don't impose any one model. Some provide examples for different subjects. Others keep copies of former students' Personal Statements for current students to look at. But there are dangers here if you follow someone else's format too closely – you want your Personal Statement to sound like you, not like someone else who applied last year. (And do remember that UCAS puts every Personal Statement through similarity detection software, so don't be tempted to use someone else's choice phrase – use your own!)

How some students went about their Personal Statements

Some found it easier than others, but they all received offers.

JAMES APPLIED TO STUDY CIVIL ENGINEERING

'I had a go at putting together my Personal Statement and found it hard to get my thoughts down on paper. After sitting staring at a blank screen for ages, waiting for the words to come into my head, I realised that I work better talking than writing. It was easier to tell someone why I wanted to do the course. Once I started to tell people what I find fascinating about civil engineering projects, the words just flowed. I was able to write down my thoughts and it sounded genuine. For some reason, I found it easier to write about playing rugby and how much I'd learnt working with others and coaching the younger teams. In the end I was pleased with my Personal Statement.'

JON APPLIED FOR HISTORY

'My brother was around when I started to think about my statement over the summer. He was already at university so he had an idea about what would work. But I didn't want him to write my statement for me - no need for that. I just found it really helpful to discuss it with someone else, to bounce ideas around. I found myself writing a bit and saving it, then I'd leave it and go and do something else. When I came back to it, I might want to change some things. It's no good rushing it - and it'll take longer than you think.'

AMIR APPLIED TO STUDY MATHS AT CAMBRIDGE

'When I wrote my Personal Statement I wanted to convince the admissions tutors how much I love maths. For me it is a real passion. My first paragraph was about how important I believe maths is in the world and that all the sciences are defined by it. In my next paragraph I wrote about my achievements in maths - the UK Maths Challenge and the British Maths Olympiad. I went on to write about my sports achievements and interests. I then returned to the subject of maths and described some books I have read about the subject.'

LUCIE APPLIED TO STUDY PSYCHOLOGY, WHICH SHE HAD NOT DONE AT A LEVEL

'I spent a lot of time on my Personal Statement - and quite a lot on cutting it down to size. I had a lot to include and it took several attempts to get the wording right. I felt it was important to impress on admissions tutors how much I had found out about the subject and how it would fit in with my career plans. I tried to write in a lively way about my work at the Me2Club with Jo, a teenage girl coping with Down's Syndrome who I've been helping integrate into the community. I used the first paragraph to describe the range of different responses Jo received and how this fuelled my desire to understand the human mind and behaviour through studying psychology. I also wrote about my other experience of working with people who have disabilities.

'In the second section I wrote about the steps I've taken to find out what the study of psychology entails and I named books and said what I found interesting in them. I stressed that I was applying for courses accredited by the British Psychological Society and said that my career aim was to become an educational psychologist.

'In a third paragraph I wrote about the aspects of each of my A level subjects that would help in studying psychology, giving examples.

'Next, I named positions of responsibility in school, sport, voluntary work and my part-time job as a waitress, drawing out the skills I had gained from each one – communication, initiative, presentation skills, teamwork, flexibility, patience and resourcefulness. I also used this paragraph to prove that I am good at managing my time, juggling all these commitments with academic work (and a prediction of high A level grades).

'The statement ended with an account of my gap-year plans and a final sentence reaffirming my motivation to do a psychology degree.'

A word of caution

The Personal Statement is such an important part of the application process that there is a brisk trade in plagiarism (copying). It is possible to find copies of Personal Statements on the internet. It has been known for applicants to use them word for word – and expect to get away with it.

It won't work. UCAS has a similarity detection service called Copycatch. Each Personal Statement sent to UCAS is checked against those already in the Copycatch system and against sample statements that have appeared in newspaper articles and on websites. The system looks for a certain level of similarity. Any statements which appear to be too similar to previous ones are reviewed. The candidate and the HEIs they have applied to are notified.

Finally

Before you send off your Personal Statement, make sure you proofread it carefully. It's a good idea to get someone else to look at it, too. Admissions tutors do take into account spelling, grammar and punctuation. If you have put a lot of effort into getting the content of your statement just right, you don't want to spoil it with careless mistakes. It may be the only sample of your written work that admissions staff see and on which they will base their judgement of your suitability for the course.

This is particularly true if you are applying for a course such as English, but treat it as just as important for all subjects.

CHAPTER SIX
ADMISSIONS TESTS

Some university departments require you to take an admission test which they will look at alongside all the other application information you submit – Personal Statement, references, grades (both achieved and predicted) – to decide whether or not to invite you for an interview and offer you a place.

Why on earth, you may ask, should you have to take special tests? After all, you spend a lot of time working for GCSEs, AS levels and A2s or equivalent qualifications – and some of you will be taking extension qualifications such as the AQA Bacc or the Cambridge Pre-U as well. The answer is that top universities receive so many applications from equally well-qualified applicants for their most popular courses that they need another way to choose between them. Many students now get straight A*s, As and distinctions. You have probably seen every August when the results are published how the media makes a lot of the fact that results are getting better each year. A level pass rates have risen every year for the past 28 years! For example, in 2010, pass rates rose (again) to 97.6%, while 27% of entries achieved an A and 8% got the newly-awarded A*. These stunning results represent a lot of hard work by students. But they can represent a headache for admissions tutors. How can they decide which applicants to offer places to when so many are predicted or have already achieved top grades? There just aren't enough places for everyone.

So over the years, university departments have devised tests to assess applicants' aptitude for particular courses. The tests may appear to be run by separate companies, but all have been devised by representatives from the universities who use them as part of their admission process.

There is a now a range of tests – sometimes more than one for a particular subject or subject area. Some university departments *require* a test and others *recommend* one (to add weight to your application). So it is vitally important that you know whether you have to take a test for the courses you want to apply for.

The universities and departments are very clear about whether they require a test as part of the application process. No one is trying to catch you out. The universities are trying to be sure that they are taking the best applicants, but they also want to give you the best possible chance to be among those candidates.

You may also want to be aware that there is a fee for some of these tests. However, the universities do not want the cost of the test to put people off taking it. There are schemes for help with the costs. The university departments or the test websites have further details.

MEDICINE, DENTISTRY, BIOMEDICAL SCIENCES AND VETERINARY SCIENCE

There are two tests for medicine, dentistry and veterinary courses – the BioMedical Admissions Test (BMAT) and the UK Clinical Aptitude Test (UKCAT). Most universities use one or other. So, depending on your choice of where to study, you may have to take both tests.

The BioMedical Admissions Test (BMAT)

The following universities use BMAT:

- University of Cambridge (for medicine and veterinary medicine)
- Imperial College, London (for medicine and biomedical sciences)
- University of Oxford (for medicine and biomedical sciences)
- The Royal Veterinary College, London
- UCL (for medicine).

BMAT is a two-hour test consisting of three papers.

1. Aptitude and Skills (60 minutes): 35 short answers or multiple choice, designed to test problem solving, understanding argument, data analysis and inference.

2. Scientific Knowledge and Applications (20 minutes): 27 multiple choice or short answers based on the application of knowledge from National Curriculum Key Stage 4 science and maths courses.

3   Writing Task (30 minutes): one essay question from a choice of four to test the ability to develop ideas and explain them effectively in writing.

Cambridge Assessment, which administers the BMAT, offers it each November. The date is published on its website; for 2011 courses it was 3 November 2010. You may be able to sit it at your own school or college. If not, there are open centres throughout the UK (and overseas). The results are issued within a few weeks (for 2011 entry, it was 24 November). There is a fee for the test. You can find out more on the BMAT website: www.admissionstests. cambridgeassessment.org.uk/adt/bmat/datesandcost.

The UK Clinical Aptitude Test (UKCAT)

UKCAT has been developed by a consortium of medical and dental schools. You will be asked to take the test if you apply to:

- University of Aberdeen (medicine and dentistry)
- Barts and the London School of Medicine and Dentistry (medicine and dentistry)
- Brighton and Sussex Medical School (medicine)
- Cardiff University (medicine and dentistry)
- University of Dundee (medicine and dentistry)
- Durham University (medicine)
- University of East Anglia (medicine)
- University of Edinburgh (medicine)
- University of Glasgow (medicine and dentistry)
- Hull York Medical School (medicine)
- Imperial College, London (for graduate entry) (medicine)
- Keele University (medicine)
- King's College, London (medicine and dentistry)
- University of Leeds (medicine)
- University of Leicester (medicine)
- University of Manchester (medicine and dentistry)
- Newcastle University (medicine and dentistry)
- University of Nottingham (medicine)
- University of Oxford (graduate entry medicine)
- Peninsula College of Medicine and Dentistry (medicine)
- Queen's University, Belfast (medicine and dentistry)
- St Andrews University (medicine)

- St George's, University of London (medicine)
- University of Sheffield (medicine and dentistry)
- University of Southampton (medicine and dentistry)
- University of Warwick (graduate entry medicine).

UKCAT is a two-hour online test in five sections.

1 Verbal Reasoning (22 minutes): 44 questions to test the ability to think logically about written information and to arrive at a reasoned conclusion.

2 Quantitative Reasoning (23 minutes): 36 questions to test the ability to solve numerical problems.

3 Abstract Reasoning (16 minutes): 65 questions to test the ability to infer relationships from information by convergent and divergent thinking.

4 Decision Analysis (32 minutes): 28 questions to test the ability to deal with different types of information, to infer relationships, to make informed judgements and to decide on appropriate responses in complex situations.

5 Non-cognitive Analysis (27 minutes): this looks for 'attributes and characteristics that may contribute to successful professional practice'.

Registration opens in May and the test can be taken between July and October. For 2012 entry, testing is from 5 July to 7 October 2011. You have to take the test at a Pearson Professional Centre at a work station in an individual booth, alongside other test candidates, under the supervision of a Pearson member of staff. There are centres throughout the UK (and overseas). If you have taken your driving test you will already be familiar with the set-up, as the Pearson company also administers the theory test. The UKCAT website has links to a virtual tour of a typical test centre. There is a fee for the test. Find out more on the UKCAT website: www.ukcat.ac.uk.

LAW

The National Admissions Test for Law (known as LNAT) is designed to test your aptitude for studying law, rather than your educational achievements. You will need to take this test if you apply to study law at any of the following universities:

- University of Birmingham
- University of Bristol

- Durham University
- University of Glasgow
- King's College, London
- University of Nottingham
- University of Oxford
- UCL.

The University of Cambridge no longer uses LNAT. It has devised its own test for law courses (more details below).

LNAT is a two-part online test that takes two-and-a-quarter hours.

1 Section A (95 minutes): 42 multiple choice questions based on 12 argumentative passages, with three or four questions on each passage.

2 Section B (40 minutes): one of five essay questions to test the ability to argue to a conclusion using good English.

Both parts are designed to assess your skills in:

- comprehension
- analysis
- interpretation
- synthesis
- induction
- deduction.

You have to take the test at a Pearson Professional Centre at a work station in an individual booth, alongside other test candidates, under the supervision of a Pearson member of staff. The LNAT website has a full list of centres throughout the UK and overseas. If you have taken your driving test you will already be familiar with the set-up, as Pearson also administers the theory test. The LNAT website has links to a virtual tour of a typical test centre.

You can register for LNAT from 1 August and take the test from 1 September. LNAT recommends booking and taking the test early, particularly if you are applying to Oxford, so you can meet the UCAS deadlines. You can, however, sit LNAT right through the academic year (until the end of June) if you are making a late application. There is a fee for the test.

There is more information on the LNAT website, www.lnat.ac.uk, which has information about the different parts of the test, hints and tips, practice questions and sample essays.

OTHER TESTS

As well as BMAT, LNAT and UKCAT, there are other less widely used tests. Oxford and Cambridge, in particular, have a tradition of using admissions tests but, as you can see below, other universities are using them for their popular courses. Some have been devised for or by particular departments, and others are used across departments. Some cover several subjects and others are very subject specific. It is up to individual university departments (and colleges in the case of Oxford and Cambridge) rather than being a university-wide decision. Departments and colleges also vary in the way they use the tests. For some, it is part of the interview, while others use the test results as part of the selection before the interview stage.

Both Oxford and Cambridge are divided into colleges as well as academic departments. On the whole, admissions policies do not differ much between colleges. You need to be aware, though, that there are some small differences.

Cambridge's tests are as follows:

- Law Test
- Thinking Skills Assessment
- Modern and Medieval Languages Test (MML).

Oxford, meanwhile, has the following tests:

- English Literature Admissions Test (ELAT)
- History Aptitude Test (HAT)
- Language Tests and Language Aptitude Tests
- Maths Admission Test
- Thinking Skills Assessment
- Physics Aptitude Test.

Other admissions tests are:

- Sixth Term Examination Paper (STEP): required for Cambridge and Warwick, and recommended by several others (see below)
- UCL Thinking Skills Assessment.

Cambridge Law Test

This is used by most Cambridge colleges as part of the admissions process for law courses. The test lasts an hour and you are asked to write one essay (using paper and pen). You sit the test while attending for interview. The college will let you know the arrangements. There is no fee. To find out more, visit www.law. cam.ac.uk/admissions/cambridge-law-test.php.

Cambridge Thinking Skills Assessment

This is required for the following courses at the University of Cambridge:

- Computer Science
- Economics
- Engineering
- Land Economy
- Natural Sciences
- Politics, Psychology and Sociology.

It is a 90-minute test, consisting of 50 multiple choice questions, designed to assess critical thinking, problem-solving skills, numerical and spatial reasoning and reasoning using everyday language. Some colleges administer it as a written test and some online. You don't need to register in advance, as the college you have applied to will tell you the arrangements. The test is taken when you attend for interview. There is no fee. Find out more on the TSA website: www. admissionstests.cambridgeassessment.org.uk/adt/tsacambridge.

Cambridge Modern and Medieval Languages Test (MML)

Some Cambridge colleges require a test for modern and medieval languages courses. In all cases, the test takes place when you attend for interview, but the test differs from college to college – some are written, others are oral and some include both. You will be told the arrangements by the college. Find out more here: www.mml.cam.ac.uk/prospectus/undergrad/test.html.

Oxford English Literature Admissions Test (ELAT)

The University of Oxford requires this test for courses which include English, such as those where English is combined with other languages (except history and English, which requires the HAT – see below).

ELAT is a 90-minute test. You are asked to write one essay question using two or three passages of set text. It is designed to allow you to show your close reading ability and expects you to take into account aspects such as language, syntax and allusion.

The test takes place on one day in November each year (for 2011 entry, it was 3 November 2010). You may be able to sit it at your own school or college. If not, there are open centres throughout the UK (and overseas). The results are issued within a few weeks. There is no fee. For more details, see: www. admissionstests.cambridgeassessment.org.uk/adt/elat/about.

Oxford History Aptitude Test (HAT)

HAT is required for all history courses at Oxford, including:

- Ancient and Modern History
- History and Economics
- History and English
- History and Modern Languages
- History and Politics.

It is a two-hour test. You are required to read two extracts and answer four questions about them. HAT takes place on a specified day each year. For 2011 entry, this was 3 November 2010. Results are issued within three to four weeks. You may be able to sit it at your own school or college. If not, there are open centres throughout the UK (and overseas). The results are issued within a few weeks. There is no fee. More information can be found at: www.history.ox.ac.uk/ prosundergrad/applying/hat_introduction.htm.

Oxford Language Tests and Language Aptitude Tests

You will have to sit a test if you are applying for any course which includes a modern or ancient foreign language. If you are already studying the language(s), you will take a test of your ability in that language (or languages). If you have never studied the language before, you will be asked to take an aptitude test.

The Language Aptitude Test is on a particular day in November. For 2011 entry, this was 3 November 2010. You can take the test at your school or college if they are willing to administer it. If not, there are open centres throughout the UK (and overseas).

Language tests are taken as part of the interview (usually December); the university will tell you the arrangements and dates. For more details, see: www.ox.ac.uk/admissions/undergraduate_courses/how_to_apply/tests/index.html.

Oxford Maths Admission Test

The university requires this test for the following courses:

- Computer Science
- Mathematics
- Mathematics with Computer Science
- Mathematics with Philosophy
- Mathematics with Statistics.

The test lasts two-and-a-half hours and includes 10 multiple choice questions followed by longer questions from which you choose four. The test is intended for all maths students, whatever syllabus they follow, and whether or not they are studying further maths. It aims to test the depth of mathematical understanding. For more details, visit www.maths.ox.ac.uk/prospective-students/undergraduate/specimen-tests.

Oxford Thinking Skills Assessment

The University of Oxford requires this test for the following courses:

- Psychology and Philosophy
- Experimental Psychology
- Economics and Management
- Philosophy, Politics and Economics.

It is a two-hour and pen-and-paper test in two parts.

1 Part 1: 50 multiple choice questions.

2 Part 2: one essay question from a choice of three.

Cambridge Assessment, which administers the Oxford Thinking Skills Assessment, offers it each November. The date is published on its website.

For 2011 courses, it was 3 November 2010. You can take the test at your school or college if they are willing to administer it. If not, there are open centres throughout the UK (and overseas). The results are issued in January (for 2011 entry, it was 14 January 2011). There is no fee. More details are available at: www.admissionstests.cambridgeassessment.org.uk/adt/tsaoxford.

Oxford Physics Aptitude Test

This test applies to all applicants for the following courses at Oxford:

- Physics
- Physics and Philosophy.

The test is a two-hour paper-and-pen test.

1 Part A is maths for physics.

2 Part B is physics and includes multiple choice, written questions and 'long questions'.

The test takes place on a particular day in November – for 2011 entry, this was 3 November 2010. There is no fee for the test. The university expects you to be able to take the test at your school or college and will send the paper to them. If it is not possible (or your school is closed on that day), you can make arrangements to take the test at another centre – the website has details of how to go about this: www.physics.ox.ac.uk/admissions/undergraduate/apptests.htm.

Sixth Term Examination Paper (STEP)

This is a maths test. It is required for applications for maths courses at:

- Cambridge
- Warwick.

The test includes courses with a strong maths element, such as engineering, computer science or natural sciences.

The following universities recommend the test for applications to maths courses:

- Bath
- Bristol

- Imperial College, London
- Oxford.

There are three, three-hour papers, each with questions on pure maths, mechanics and statistics and probability. STEP 1 and 2 are based on Maths A level and STEP 3 is based on Further Maths A level. Although STEP has three papers, universities specify which they want candidates to sit (usually one or two). The papers are designed to test your insight, originality and grasp of broader issues.

You can take the test at your school or college if they are willing to administer it. If not, there are open centres throughout the UK (and overseas). For 2011 entry, registration opened on 1 March 2011 and the exams take place on 20, 22 and 24 June 2011 (depending on which papers you sit). The results are issued in August (18 August for 2011 entry). There is a fee for taking the STEP. You can find out more at www.maths.cam.ac.uk/undergrad/admissions/step.

UCL Thinking Skills Assessment

University College, London requires applicants for the European Social and Political Studies course to sit this test. It is a paper-and-pen test lasting 90 minutes. You are asked to sit a single paper with 50 multiple choice questions. You take the test as part of your interview; you will be told the date by the admissions staff. For 2011 entry, the dates were in December 2010 and January, February and March 2011. There is no fee. Find out more by visiting: www.admissionstests.cambridgeassessment.org.uk/adt/tsaucl.

CAN YOU PREPARE FOR ADMISSION TESTS?

The tests are designed to assess your aptitude for a particular course of study – and therefore for the profession it leads to. As suggested above, none require any specialist knowledge beyond the curriculum you are studying. Where it is relevant, they are based on the syllabus of the courses you are doing anyway – A level, Higher, International Baccalaureate and so on. The universities are looking for the way you apply this knowledge and whether you can think logically and clearly and present reasoned arguments.

What do the test organisations say themselves? LNAT says the test 'cannot be revised for', BMAT says it 'cannot be crammed for' and UKCAT says 'coaching is not necessary, desirable or advantageous'. The Oxford Thinking Skills Assessment suggests that you 'think carefully' before paying for test preparation.

Nevertheless, there are organisations who claim to be able to prepare you for these tests – with classroom courses, online courses or private tuition. Needless to say, all have to be paid for. Two-day classroom courses, for example, are around £250 and five hours' private tutoring can be nearly £500.

While the test organisations consider this sort of preparation unnecessary and possibly a waste of money, it would be very unwise to approach any of these tests without doing *some* preparation. Here are some useful things that you can do.

- Find out as much as you can about the tests. I have given you a basic outline here, but there is published information for each test about its format, the time allowed, the type of questions and what it is designed to assess. You will be familiar with the layout of the test papers on online screens when it is your turn to sit the test. It is worth knowing, for example, the word count allowed for essay questions.
- Do some practice papers or look at past papers.
- Talk to the people who know. You should be supported by your school or college in your HEI applications. If so, it is likely that one of your teachers or tutors has helped students through the process before. If you are the first from your school or college (or family) to take one of the tests, you may need to do more of the research yourself. You don't need to let this put you off – the information is all there on the websites, clearly laid out. You will be developing investigative skills which will be useful once you get to university and beyond.
- Talk to people who've done the test before – students in the years above you at school or college, maybe, or family or friends. If you don't know anyone who's done the test you're planning to take, trying putting the name of the test into your search engine. There are message boards and forums where you can talk to people in your situation. (Remember, though, that the tests change from time to time, so anyone who did the test in the past may have used a slightly different version from the one you will face.)

- Be organised. Make sure you know whether you have to register for the test, and if so when and how. All the information is on the test website. Be sure to register in time – late applications can be difficult, if not impossible. Registering early means you are more likely to get an early test date (where there is a choice of dates).

- If you have any special requirements – for access to a test centre or for taking the test – make sure you let the centre know in advance. Be clear about your requirements to give yourself the best chance of success. If you have special needs you are probably used to these being met for exams. Remember, though – especially if you are not taking your test at your own school or college – the test administrators will not be aware of your needs unless you tell them.

In addition, as well as making sure you are very familiar with the basics of your subject, some of the tests make specific preparation suggestions. For example:

- both the Oxford and Cambridge Thinking Skills Assessments list books on thinking skills and critical thinking
- BMAT publishes an official guide *Preparing for the BMAT*
- STEP has links to preparation websites.

ANNA TOOK THE UKCAT

'I was quite nervous about it. I found the practice questions on the UKCAT website helpful. They made me realise that you could only use the information given to work out an answer, as opposed to giving what you thought was the correct one. But you could spend more time on them than in the actual test. As a result, I felt under constant pressure during the real thing and I had to do the last 20 questions very quickly. I had only just reached the last question when a message saying that time was up appeared on the screen.

'At the test centre, I was shown into a waiting room where the invigilator gave us each a locker for all our personal belongings. You are not allowed to take anything in with you. He then explained what would happen and we could see through a glass wall into the room where some people were already doing the test, working at individual computer stations and wearing headphones. We each had a small whiteboard in case we wanted to work anything out and each computer had its own calculator.

'Each section of the test had a briefing page which you could read at your own pace but as soon as you keyed "Next" the timer started and you had to go straight into the questions.'

MARIA TOOK THE BMAT AS PART OF HER APPLICATION FOR VETERINARY SCIENCE

'I sat the test at school with people applying for medicine. It helped to be in familiar surroundings. My advice when you're taking the test is to stay chilled - and don't overthink. It's more straightforward than I expected. Stay calm for the multiple choice, as some of the questions seem designed to confuse.'

OTHER ASSESSMENTS

Written work

In some subjects, admissions tutors ask for samples of written work. Again, this is particularly true of Oxford and Cambridge and may be instead of or as well as admissions tests. Typically you will be asked to send one or two pieces of work, marked by your teachers – usually work done as a normal part of your course. Be prepared to discuss at your interview the work you have submitted (so keep a copy!).

Other HEIs which ask for pieces of work include:

- UCL's Department of English asks some applicants to complete one or two written exercises in order to decide whether or not to ask them for interview
- London College of Communication (part of the University of the Arts) asks interview candidates for the journalism degree to submit pieces of work.

HEI departments give full details on their web pages if they require you to submit work. If you know that the course(s) you want to apply to may ask you to submit material, you should work with your tutors and subject teachers to select the pieces of work that will show you in your best light, demonstrating the range of your work – in terms of breadth and depth.

CHAPTER SEVEN
INTERVIEWS AND AUDITIONS

You may or may not be asked to attend an interview at any or all of the HEIs you have applied to. There is not usually an HEI-wide policy on interviews – staff in individual departments normally make the decision. Some interview all applicants. Some do an initial sift and interview all candidates who meet minimum requirements and some interview borderline applicants.

So don't be surprised if you are invited to an interview and your friends aren't – or the other way round – either at the same HEI or at a different one, or even if you've applied for the same course. This is neither a good sign nor a bad one, or any reflection on either of you. It is simply a matter of policy. Many HEIs simply don't use interviews as part of their selection process. Rachel, studying Biomedical Science at Lancaster, received offers from each of her five choices without being invited to any interviews. On the other hand Sarah, studying Graphic Design at Leeds College of Art, had five interviews, all in February.

NICK PHILLIPS, HEAD OF ACTING AND COMMUNITY DRAMA, LIPA
'We receive up to 2,500 applications for our 34 places. We find it useful to audition all the candidates who meet our minimum criteria. We have found from experience that screening can mean we miss some excellent candidates, so would rather call them for auditions and make our offers based on what we see.'

KIERON SALMON, DIRECTOR OF ADMISSIONS, THE SCHOOL OF VETERINARY SCIENCE, UNIVERSITY OF LIVERPOOL
'Of the 1,500-1,600 applications we receive each year, about 1,000 meet our requirements. After we've scored the applications, we invite the top 500 candidates for interview.'

PAUL BAINES, HEAD OF THE SCHOOL OF ENGLISH, UNIVERSITY OF LIVERPOOL

'We receive over 800 applications, sometimes as many as 1,200, so we feel it would be impractical to conduct interviews.'

JONATHAN HOGG, ADMISSIONS OFFICER, SCHOOL OF HISTORY, UNIVERSITY OF LIVERPOOL

'We don't interview our applicants because we have found we don't need to. We are getting enough high-calibre candidates and can make offers without seeing them.'

EXCEPTIONAL CASES

Even departments which do not routinely invite applicants for interview may interview:

- mature candidates
- applicants with a non-standard educational background
- 'borderline cases', whose predicted grades may not be as high as the entry requirements dictate but who have very supportive references.

Other than those in the above categories you are more likely to be interviewed if you are applying:

- for a new subject (one you have not studied before)
- for a vocational course which forms the first part of the necessary training
- to Oxford or Cambridge.

WHAT HAPPENS IN AN INTERVIEW?

This varies. As with the decision whether or not to conduct interviews, HEIs and their departments have different ways of carrying out interviews. If you have an interview, it could be

- one to one
- with two people
- in front of a panel.

The number and format of interviews varies, too. You could have just one interview or more than one. Two interviews is quite a common pattern. In some cases, you have a series of interviews. It may sound daunting to think you might be interviewed by two or more people at once, but it can make it a less intense experience than a one-to-one interview. Likewise, having more than one interview or being interviewed by more than one person can be tiring, but it ends up being a fairer process, as the HEI will have more than one person's opinion of you on which to base their decision.

VANDA FENN, FACULTY ACADEMIC ADMISSIONS CO-ORDINATOR, SCHOOL OF HEALTH AND SOCIAL CARE, UNIVERSITY OF THE WEST OF ENGLAND, BRISTOL

'Most interviews are conducted by two people. We think that is fairer to the students.'

The person (or people) who interview you may be any or all of the following:

- admission tutors
- academic staff
- people from outside the HEI

or even

- students.

Yes, you may be interviewed by students!

EILEEN THEIL, ADMISSIONS TUTOR, THE SCHOOL OF DENTISTRY, UNIVERSITY OF LIVERPOOL

'We have two or three people on our interview panels, including people from outside the university such as dental practitioners, teachers and heads. It is valuable to us and we think it also gives teachers an insight into what we are looking for, which can help when they are advising their students. An interview panel may also include senior students whom we have trained in interviewing.'

KIERON SALMON, DIRECTOR OF ADMISSIONS, THE SCHOOL OF VETERINARY SCIENCE, UNIVERSITY OF LIVERPOOL

'We run a system of multiple mini-interviews - "speed interviewing", perhaps. Each candidate has nine five-minute interviews across seven different topics. For us it's all about the communication skills which they will need when they are vets, working with the owners of the animals.'

If this sounds daunting, here's what a student says:

MARIA IS A STUDENT AT THE SCHOOL OF VETERINARY SCIENCE, THE UNIVERSITY OF LIVERPOOL

'I found the whole interview a good process - comfortable and relaxed. I felt that if one person didn't like me, then I had a chance with the others.'

Sometimes, interviews are combined with open days, giving you a chance to look round the HEI and talk to current students. In some cases, the selection process includes practical assessments, group exercises, discussions and debates as well as one or more interviews.

ANNA, A MEDICAL STUDENT, ALSO HAD EXPERIENCE OF THIS STYLE OF INTERVIEW

'In the interview room, there were seven stations to move through, spending five or six minutes at each. In between, we all went back to our seats for a minute or two while the interviewers graded our performance on score sheets. We went to all the stations in turn. Some of the questions involved scenarios - one was about how to help a friend who was under pressure and another was about a patient who was not taking prescribed medication. At other stations I was asked why they should select me, why I had chosen to apply there, about my ability to work in a team and about my work experience.'

JAMES HAD AN INTERVIEW AND ASSESSMENT FOR CIVIL ENGINEERING AT UCL

'It was described as an introductory day for the course. They told me I would be there for a few hours. I could choose a day, so I chose one which meant missing the fewest lessons. I wasn't really nervous, I'm used to travelling and going to London, but I had to ask someone for directions to the right building.

'There were 30 of us, divided into groups of six. First, we had a tour with our two group leaders - a third year and a Master's student. They showed us all the UCL buildings, including the gym. After refreshments, our leaders explained the task to us: a town is built on cliffs which are receding - what can we do about it? We had 20 minutes to discuss the task and plan a presentation. I think it was a test of our engineering and thinking skills, rather than our knowledge, as well as looking at how we worked in a group. We were observed by a tutor taking notes. One by one we were taken aside to talk about our Personal Statements.'

DIVYA ALSO HAD SOME PRACTICAL ASSESSMENTS WHEN SHE APPLIED FOR CIVIL ENGINEERING

'Imperial College, London was the most technical. In the morning the candidates were divided into groups of four and set projects to do. In the afternoon I had a

25-minute interview with a geotechnics specialist. The interviewer was very nice and started by asking me some general questions like my reasons for choosing the course and the place, then moved on to ask me things related to the morning project. She then asked some technical questions on physics. At Bath, the one-to-one interview was part of a departmental open day. We had a campus tour, saw the accommodation and had lunch. There was a problem-solving exercise here too. This time, working in small groups we had to construct a tower out of drinking straws and Blu-Tack that would support a given weight.'

Interview format

There is no standard interview format. Some interviews are very informal. Most people say that the interviewers were friendly and helped them to feel at ease.

An interviewer may begin by asking you about some of the things you wrote on your Personal Statement. This is designed to be within your comfort zone. You know what you wrote and can expand on this to provide further information. Very often, the whole interview is based around the Personal Statement and follows it closely. It is absolutely vital to remember what you wrote!

Interviewers may ask technical questions, possibly on some aspects of your exam syllabus. The questions may be designed to go beyond what you have studied already or make you think a problem through. Usually, as well as being interested in your responses the interviewer is looking at the ways in which you think and your reasoning to reach an answer. Often there are no right or wrong answers, as Anna found when she had her interview for medicine:

'The scenario was about advising a pregnant patient with a strong chance of giving birth to a baby with a handicap whether or not to have a test carried out. The procedure would contain a risk of miscarriage. I first said that I would give the patient all the information as clearly and compassionately as I could and leave the decision to her - but they said that I had to offer advice. So I said that I thought that the test should be advised. The doctor then said to me "How would you feel if the baby died?" so I thought I must have given the wrong answer. However, I discovered later he had asked another applicant who had given the opposite answer how she would feel if the baby was born with a severe handicap.'

Some typical interview questions are as follows.

- Why do you want to come here?
- Why should we give you a place?
- Are you a leader?
- Can you work in a team?
- Give me an example of something that you have achieved in the past year.
- Have you been to one of our open days?
- What have you read outside the A level syllabus?
- Why did you have a poor grade in GCSE Maths/French/Geography etc.?
- What do you do in your spare time?
- What skills have you learnt from your part-time employment?
- Tell us some more about your work experience at X.
- Tell me more about the drama group/hockey team/Saturday job you wrote about on your application.
- Have you any questions for us?

Interviews always include the opportunity for you to ask questions. It is a good idea to have some ready. There is nothing wrong with writing them down and taking the list with you. Try not to ask anything that you could have found out from the website or prospectus. It is quite all right, though, to ask about or discuss something from the website – to find out more about the methods of assessment or staff research interests, maybe, or links with particular employers.

Asking questions is a good way of showing your interest in the subject or department, so prepare some if you possibly can. If you find that your questions have already been answered you can say so: 'Thank you. I did have questions about X, Y and Z but they have been answered today.'

To prove that you have done thorough research about the course, you can always say something like 'No thank you, your website was very detailed and gave me all the information I need' (flattering) or 'I spoke to someone about the course at your open day and had all my questions answered then' (proves you have been thinking about this course for some time).

Some typical course- or subject-related questions are as follows (subjects are given in brackets where not clear otherwise).

- Why do you want to do this subject/be a barrister/be a doctor?
- What qualities do you think a successful doctor/engineer/surveyor should have? Do you possess them?
- Have you read about any legal cases in the last few weeks?
- What is the role of the architect in society?
- What changes in the landscape did you notice on your journey here? (geography, environmental studies)
- What transport problems are there in your local area? (planning, geography)
- What stereotypes do we have about people with mental illness? (psychology)
- What is a philosophical question?
- Have any important advances been made in the biological field recently?
- Should nurses have the right to strike?
- How would you feel if you had to promote a product that you did not personally like? (advertising, marketing)
- What causes a volcano?
- What do you think of the selection of novels made for the last Booker Prize?
- Is the power of the prime minister increasing? (politics)
- Describe a recent practical you carried out (sciences).
- What makes a good manager? (business studies).

What you will not get are any trick questions. Interviewers do not try to catch you out. They are trying to get to know you as a person. They are trying to assess whether you:

- will be able to cope academically with the course
- are sufficiently interested in it
- have the right personal qualities, especially for vocational courses
- have the right practical or technical skills
- will benefit from the course.

Interviewers are not looking for reasons to reject candidates. They simply want the right students on their courses. It is in nobody's interests, least of all students', to be given places on courses they will not cope with or enjoy. They will only drop out. Interviewers may have a checklist of points to look for, such as:

- did the candidate maintain eye contact throughout the interview?
- was s/he enthusiastic and well-motivated?
- does s/he communicate well?
- did s/he demonstrate commitment to the subject?
- has s/he taken steps to find out about X as a career?

FRED LOEBINGER, ADMISSIONS TUTOR, THE DEPARTMENT OF PHYSICS AND ASTRONOMY, UNIVERSITY OF MANCHESTER

'We use a range of staff for interviews. The style of interview and questions are left up to the individual member of staff. They all fill in a standard interview feedback questionnaire asking, for example, whether their impression of the applicant matches that of the school.'

A new subject

If you are applying for a subject that you have not done before, admissions tutors need to be sure that you understand what you are letting yourself in for. You could be invited to an interview and asked questions designed to find out just how much you know about the subject and what steps you took to find out.

ALEX IS STUDYING TRANSPORTATION DESIGN AT NORTHUMBRIA UNIVERSITY

'I was interviewed by a lecturer who had worked in the car industry (and is now my personal tutor). When he asked me about my reasons for wanting to do the course, I did my best to explain how exciting I found design work. I tried hard to avoid phrases like "I have loved cars forever." We also talked about my interest in cars but more specifically in yacht design. It turned out that he loved boats and yachts too so he asked me a lot of questions to test my knowledge. Luckily I was able to mention names of companies and explain why I admire their products. He looked through my portfolio too, of course, and asked me a lot of questions about why I had chosen certain topics, why I had done the pieces in a particular way and so on. It was a very relaxed atmosphere, though, an enjoyable experience in fact, and I felt as though I was chatting to a fellow enthusiast.'

PREPARING FOR INTERVIEWS

Some ways to prepare include:

- being very clear about why you want to study the subject at that particular HEI (remember that you may well give different answers at different interviews!)
- reading widely around your chosen subject
- being ready to talk about something that is outside or deeper than your A level syllabus
- reading newspaper articles, websites, professional journals and magazines
- reading a quality national newspaper and being informed about current affairs – especially those relevant to your subject or course.

It is also worth re-reading your Personal Statement and any written work that you had to send in and being prepared to be questioned on it.

Practice interviews

It can be a good idea to find someone who will hold a practice interview with you. If it is for an academic subject, the ideal person would be someone who teaches that subject but who does not teach you. That way you will be talking with a subject expert but will also be getting used to doing so with a stranger.

A course that is directly linked to a particular career

This usually also comes into the 'new subject' category, and includes courses such as architecture, law, medicine, engineering and those leading to qualifications in caring or health care professions.

Here, the interviewer is assessing students for the ability not only to succeed on a particular course but also to work in the relevant profession. They will be looking for specific skills and qualities – and the interview may include some questions related to that career. Often, a person working in that profession may be one of the interviewers. Frequently, a short interview is only a small part of a selection day or half-day in which students have to do some practical tests and assessments.

VANDA FENN, FACULTY ACADEMIC ADMISSIONS CO-ORDINATOR, SCHOOL OF HEALTH AND SOCIAL CARE, UNIVERSITY OF THE WEST OF ENGLAND, BRISTOL

'Two people, one a member of the school's academic staff and the other a practising midwife, conduct the interviews, which are based on candidates' past experiences. They will ask questions such as "What have you done as part of a team?" or "Can you describe a situation in which you had to deal with someone who was behaving angrily or aggressively towards you?" Both interviewers score the candidate's performance and successful applicants are offered places.'

Preparation of portfolios has been mentioned in Chapter 4. You may be asked to send in such a portfolio or take it to the interview, where you will be expected to discuss your work.

JOE STATHERS-TRACEY, HEAD OF THEATRE AND PERFORMANCE DESIGN AND THEATRE AND PERFORMANCE TECHNOLOGY AT LIPA

'At interviews, the questions are designed to draw out the candidate's aptitude for live work. We expect them to use their portfolio to demonstrate this. For the design course we are looking for a range of skills in design and fine art, together with a passion for live work in theatre or fashion. We need to see a broad range of work and expect you to show your personality and enthusiasm and be able to articulate why LIPA is the right place for you.

'For performance technology, the portfolio may include photos as well as plans and schedules from work you have done. Photos can be appropriate, even for sound work, if they show the challenges you faced, especially in non-theatre performance spaces. We don't expect professional experience - we are talking about school, college, church or other live events.'

Some more students' experiences

ANNA, MEDICAL STUDENT, DURHAM UNIVERSITY

'Durham was where I had decided I really wanted to go and I would much rather have had an interview somewhere else first for the practice! The interview wasn't quite what I had expected. It was with the admissions secretary of the medical school and a local doctor. They hadn't seen my UCAS application so they knew nothing about me. This is the standard practice there and they explained to me that it was in order to stop them feeling any prejudice or bias.

'They asked me some of the questions I had been expecting, like why I wanted to be a doctor, why I had chosen Durham, why I felt they should offer me a place, what qualities I thought a doctor should possess, but not much on my A level subjects, on science or on current issues - all of which I had been asked in my mock interview. They also asked for an example of my teamwork skills - I used netball for this - and to describe a situation I had found difficult. I didn't want to sound negative, so I thought quickly and said that I had found settling in to sixth form college quite hard but that I had persevered.

'Then there were two scenario questions. I had to read a card with the interviewers watching me and I found this quite hard. I then had to say what I would do with the information.'

JULIE IS STUDYING DIAGNOSTIC RADIOGRAPHY AT CANTERBURY CHRIST CHURCH UNIVERSITY

'At Canterbury the selection process lasted all day. First we had an introductory talk and a guided tour of the department, then a practical test. We were shown into a room where ten X-rays were laid out on tables. We had to examine them all and write descriptions of what we had found out from them. This was a test both of powers of observation and of written communication skills. After lunch we sat and waited to be called for our individual interviews. This was the most nerve-wracking part of the day.

'In my interview, which was with one of the senior lecturers, I was asked about my reasons for wanting to do radiography. I expanded on some of the things I had written on my Personal Statement and explained that I had first become interested in the profession when I had had MRI and CT scans following an accident. I had seen the job from the patient's viewpoint then and had arranged to visit a radiography department later to learn more about the work.

'I also said that I thought I had the right skills for the job. I had worked in retail both as a sales assistant and a manager, and as a care officer with people with Down's Syndrome and autism. I talked about how my experience had developed my communication and caring skills.

'The interview at City was very different. After the introductory talk, two students, one from each branch of radiography, came in to describe their own specialism and then answer questions. We had a tour of the department and were able to handle the X-ray machinery, then had two practical tests before the individual interviews. First we did an observation and communication exercise. The part that I enjoyed most was a short debate. We all had to pick a topic out of a hat and speak on the subject for five minutes. Mine was equality and lasted for 10 minutes because once I had started it went very well and I generated a very lively discussion!'

An academic subject

If you want to study an academic subject, whether this is a familiar one such as English, geography, history or maths or one new to you such as philosophy, you might not have an interview. It is quite likely that a decision will be made using your exam predictions, reference and Personal Statement.

If you are interviewed, however, expect most of the questions to be on the subject and be ready to demonstrate the key qualities again. The interviewer could well be teaching you next year and will be looking for the ideal student – someone who is burning to study this particular subject in depth and who will make a positive contribution to class discussion.

 SOME INTERVIEW TIPS

Before the interview

Do . . .

- keep a hard copy of your UCAS application and re-read it just before or on your way to the interview

- make notes on anything that has changed. For example, did you mention that you were in the process of arranging some work experience but in fact were unable to do so? Be ready to explain that it didn't come off but that you tried very hard

- if anything in your exam work has changed be ready to talk about that too. For instance, have you decided not to complete that extra AS subject?

- find out how to get to the HEI from the station or where you can park if going by car

- allow plenty of time to get there – more than you think is necessary

- if something beyond your control delays your journey – late train, motorway hold-up, accident etc. – phone and explain

◪ get there early. You can then find the interview room without getting flustered and can sit down and try to relax

◪ expect to feel nervous. Everyone does, and interviewers make allowances for nerves.

At the interview

Do . . .

◪ speak clearly

◪ answer the question that is asked, even if you would like to show what you know about the topic. It's the same advice you are given about answering exam questions, isn't it?

◪ if you don't understand the question don't be afraid to ask the interviewer to repeat or rephrase it

◪ if there is more than one person conducting the interview, maintain eye contact with the person who asked you the question but from time to time glance at the other person, too, to include them.

Don't . . .

◪ try to answer a question too quickly

◪ answer just 'yes' or 'no'

◪ talk too much. If you give a clear and concise answer, the interviewers can decide whether that is sufficient or if they want more. If so, they will continue on this topic. Let them steer the conversation

◪ criticise your school or college. If you had three changes of teacher last year this should be mentioned in your reference and they will have noted this. If you want to comment on the situation, mention the facts, but don't moan

◪ bluff. If you really don't know the answer to a question it is better to admit it. Otherwise you will get into difficulties if the questions become more detailed

◪ pretend you know about something when you don't. It could end up being very embarrassing!

OXFORD OR CAMBRIDGE

These two universities make extensive use of the interview process despite their large numbers of applicants. Why? Because both receive applications from exceptionally able candidates with predicted top grades, usually very supportive references and very good Personal Statements. Therefore they find it extremely difficult to choose between applicants fairly just on the basis of a UCAS application. Each university is keen to find the best and most suitable students – the ones who will both benefit from and contribute to the course.

As described in Chapter 6, you may be asked to sit a test when you attend for interview – arrangements differ between colleges and departments. Here are a few examples.

- Applicants to study fine art at Oxford (at the Ruskin School of Drawing and Fine Art) are asked to complete two pieces in a variety of media at their interview (as well as sending in a portfolio).
- Some Cambridge colleges ask applicants for economics to sit a maths test at interview and others a subject-based test.
- Applicants for Architecture at Cambridge may be set a written/ drawing exercise to complete at home (as well as showing a portfolio of work).

Any tests during interviews may be in addition to submitting work in advance, or may be instead of it. It is essential to check which applies to the subject and/or college you are applying to. Each university has a comprehensive section about interviews on their website, including dates and some advice on what to expect and how to prepare.

STEVE WATTS, ENGLISH LECTURER AND ADMISSIONS TUTOR, HOMERTON COLLEGE, CAMBRIDGE

'Applicants for English are sometimes given a written test; sometimes an oral test within the interview when they are asked to read through a passage, then answer questions on it. The written test might consist of comparing and contrasting two poems - as could happen in an English class here. At Homerton, candidates for English are given one hour to read a passage and then write a practical criticism (commentary) on it. The answers are marked immediately by some tutors while others begin the first of the two interviews.

'Interviews for arts subjects are based on discussion. We also discuss the written work, from which we can assess the ability to write under pressure. We usually ask for a list of books they have read recently that have made a real impact on them and ask them to explain why. If they say that it was a good book - how do they define "good"? Was it purely the subject matter that interested them? They will probably be asked questions about texts they have mentioned in their Personal Statements. I might well ask them about the texts they have not mentioned, but have studied, as well and ask them to explain why. Is it because they do not like them? Why not?

'At least 50% of interview time will be spent in taking students out of their comfort zone and forcing them to think more deeply about issues.'

Some students' experiences

AMIR APPLIED TO STUDY MATHS AT CAMBRIDGE

'I prepared for the interview by thinking of the types of questions I might be asked and I also read the file that my college keeps for us to use. Every student who attends an interview is asked to write about it and put their account in the file. I spent one day in Cambridge and had two interviews, each with one person. The first one was concerned with my knowledge. He gave me a couple of problems to solve and watched me do them. He was looking at my ability to answer questions and my analytical ability. He also went through one question with me, getting to the solution in a different way, and watched how quickly I could the same.

'The second interview was not so mathematically challenging. He said that he was interested in how my mind worked. One question was about integrating sin 5x with respect to x from pi to minus pi. Instead of using De Moivre's theorem, I realised what he was getting at and that the answer is 0.

'I was also asked "Why do you want to study maths and why here?" and "Which field of maths are you particularly interested in?"

'I was a little bit nervous before the interviews. The worst bit was waiting outside the interview room with all the other candidates. Nobody said very much. When I got inside I found that I was able to relax and concentrate on maths.'

HANNAH IS STUDYING ANGLO-SAXON NORSE AND CELTIC AT CAMBRIDGE

'I chose to travel to Cambridge the night before the interview so I wouldn't be stressed by the journey. I stayed in college accommodation where we were looked after by current students.

'I had a subject interview with the Director of Studies and an admissions tutor. The questions were mainly from my Personal Statement. I was surprised that I was not asked more history. For example, one question was "What makes a good king?". If I got stuck, they would rephrase a question to help me. The interviewer for the general interview was not from my subject so I had to tell him about it. He also asked me about my extra-curricular activities, so I was glad I could tell him about my music and sailing. My interviews were one after another with no waiting around. That made it easier.

'I would say the whole thing is worthwhile - even if you don't get in, you've had the experience of a tough interview.'

KATRINA IS STUDYING BIOLOGY AT OXFORD

'I travelled on the Sunday night so I was there ready for Monday when there were meetings for all the applicants. We were told, amongst other things, not to tell anyone else what we were asked in the interview - it would only give them an advantage over us!

'I had one interview on the Monday and another on the Tuesday, so there was a lot of hanging around. The college lays on games and films, activities designed to be diverting and fun and, OK, there are other people in the same position but nobody really knows anyone else. Although everyone is friendly, we are aware that we are in competition with each other. I found it essentially a lonely experience.

'The interview felt tough. I was put off by the fact that it was in a room like a living room - I found that disconcerting.

'Staying in college was interesting. The rooms seemed very big and empty, with no personal things around. It seems as though you've getting a taste of college life, but when I started here I realised that when you're here for your interview, it's nothing like the real thing.'

MATTHEW IS STUDYING PHYSICS AT MERTON COLLEGE, OXFORD

'I was quite nervous but I had had a mock interview at college and I knew what to expect. I found the whole thing was a good experience. Everyone was very relaxed and friendly – even the other candidates. Technically, of course, we were in competition with each other but we all got on very well.

'I had three separate interviews and in each one I was asked about topics I hadn't done before. I was given questions, for instance, on aspects of mechanics, energy or friction that were new to me. In all three interviews I could tell that the interviewers were trying to assess how I dealt with a question, how I thought things through to a conclusion and how good my analytical ability was. It wasn't so much that my answer was important – rather, how I got to it. The interviews were really like mini tutorials. I was led through the exercise by the tutors, who questioned me and added points for me to consider. They wanted to see how I responded to them and whether I could take them on board.'

 INTERVIEW TIPS

- Try not to give vague answers such as 'I like reading' (what do you read and why?).

- Best to avoid 'I like socialising' (who doesn't!).

It is far easier to give examples of bad answers than good! Good answers are personal to you – and must demonstrate the commitment, passion and enthusiasm that admissions staff are looking for.

The following are not considered good replies!

- I have seen a lot of programmes about law on television.
- My subject teacher said I should do this.
- I had a bad teacher.
- That part of the course was boring.
- It's a long time since we covered that topic.
- I've forgotten.

- I want to heal the sick.
- Your department has a good reputation (unless you can expand on this).

What to wear

If in doubt, go for smart-casual. There is no need to go out and buy an interview suit. Academic staff at HEIs are not likely to be wearing them either.

Students say:

> It really did not matter. I went to my two interviews wearing a shirt, trousers and black shoes. I saw some people who were wearing suits and others who were much more casual. The important thing is to wear something you feel comfortable in.

> For my first two interviews I wore my school skirt and sweater. It doesn't look obviously like a school uniform as it has no badges or logos and I felt that it looked smart. By the third one I was really noticing what everyone else wore and saw that it didn't actually matter. Nobody was very formal. So from then on I wore smart jeans with a decent top. I think the key is to wear something that you are comfortable in and something that won't annoy the interviewer by being too extreme.

More interview tips from students

> Before an interview, practise answers to the more obviously likely questions. When you give your reasoning for choosing a course at a given university, be sure to give an example of something they offer that others do not. This is a way of proving that you have done your research properly.

❝ Preparing answers to lots of possible questions and having a practice interview with my college's vice-principal gave me some confidence. ❞

❝ Be sure that you remember exactly what you put on your Personal Statement. All three of my interviewers used it as a structure and based the interview around it. ❞

❝ Don't lie or exaggerate anything. You will be found out! ❞

❝ In the group task, I tried to be myself. ❞

❝ It is absolutely paramount to be sure that you want to be a radiographer. If not, you will end up hating every minute of the course. You must also be able to convince admissions tutors that you have done some research into the work, so you need to spend some time observing practice and talking to radiographers. The two branches of the profession are very different and suit different people. You need to be able to convince the interviewers that you understand the difference and have chosen the branch that you are suited to. ❞

❝ I felt they were looking at our skills within a group as well as us as individuals. I was fairly vocal, as I felt everyone else was quiet, though I tried to bring them in and ask their opinions. ❞

❝ It is worth pushing yourself outside your comfort zone. When two people were asked to present the group's solution to the tutor, I volunteered, even though I really don't like public speaking. ❞

AUDITIONS

Drama

NICK PHILLIPS, HEAD OF ACTING AND COMMUNITY DRAMA, LIPA

'Our auditions are to test applicants' suitability for this course, not to seek the most talented actors – it's not The X Factor!'

If you apply for music or drama performance courses you may have one or more interviews and there will certainly be at least one audition. If successful, you will be recalled for further auditions. This may be all on one day or on several different days – which may be weeks or months apart. The Royal Academy of Dramatic Art (RADA), for example, has a four-stage process:

1 preliminary auditions between October and April

2 recall auditions from December to May

3 short workshops

4 workshop day.

LIPA auditions in the morning and successful candidates are asked to stay in the afternoon for the recall.

 We see 100 people on each audition day; perhaps 10 or 20 are recalled in the afternoon. **,**

NICK PHILLIPS, LIPA

Some schools expect applicants to travel to the school for the auditions and others hold auditions in various locations across the UK (and overseas).

Drama schools vary in what they ask applicants to prepare as audition pieces, but each is very clear about what it wants. For example, Bristol Old Vic Theatre School asks for two prepared pieces (no longer than two minutes each) and a song, for the initial audition.

Expect to audition in front of a panel, which may include students.

> We include third-year students in the audition process as they need to be able to recognise those who need further technical training and articulate their views.
>
> **NICK PHILLIPS, LIPA**

There is usually a fee – either for the application or for the audition.

> We charge a fee as the process is very labour-intensive. We hope candidates find it a valuable experience and useful for other auditions.
>
> **NICK PHILLIPS, LIPA**

Music

Music candidates have one or more auditions on one day. Expect a panel with two or more people. The audition could last between 15 and 30 minutes, although piano auditions at some places take 45 minutes. You will normally be expected to perform two contrasting pieces. Some conservatoires specify the pieces, some have a list for you to choose from or give free choice. Applicants for composition may be asked to send in advance copies of a set number of contrasting, fully notated pieces or recordings.

In addition to your audition pieces, you could expect to do any of the following:

- play a further short solo piece, which you will have been given a copy of one hour before your audition
- complete short sight-reading exercises
- improvise
- complete technical tests including scales and arpeggios
- have an aural skills assessment – often in a group of applicants completing the assessment at the same time.

The forms of assessment vary. Each conservatoire is very clear about what is required. You will have a chance to warm up before your audition starts.

For drama, and for music where there is a choice of audition pieces, the pieces need to be carefully chosen to show the full range of your ability. For example, at LIPA the audition pieces are:

- a Shakespearean speech chosen from a list
- a song
- a devised piece.

NICK PHILLIPS, HEAD OF ACTING AND COMMUNITY DRAMA, LIPA

'In the devised piece we are looking for you to communicate something you want us to know about you that you think isn't being shown elsewhere. Part of the acting course is about creating work. I know some people find this hard to do and an off-putting part of our auditions. We ask applicants to sing because music is an integral part of the course.'

ESTHER DIX, THIRD-YEAR ACTING STUDENT, LIPA

'I picked the Shakespeare piece I most liked the story of. I chose a song from the musical theatre repertoire. It's important to remember that singing is about acting, too. The piece I devised was semi-autobiographical. If you are recalled in the afternoon, you will perform a sample of your pieces in front of a panel of six or eight people and take part in a workshop with students and staff.'

ESTHER ALSO HAS SOME TIPS FOR HOW TO APPROACH AUDITIONS

'Don't try to impress or be what you think other people want you to be. You can only be yourself. Whatever you do, don't appear desperate! Be professional, approach it like a working audition. Be polite and friendly. Remember you've paid for the audition so it's your time to use. Do what you need to do to be comfortable - it's OK for your parents to go along with you. Relax! Breathe and focus - and don't apologise.'

CHAPTER EIGHT
OFFERS AND REJECTIONS

From the time that UCAS applications are submitted and passed on to the HEIs, admission tutors start to look at the applications to decide who to offer a place to. HEIs (and departments) vary enormously in the way they do this so you could receive offers any time from October to March.

Offers (and rejections) can come quickly or take some time. This may or may not be related to how soon you submitted your UCAS application. Please don't get anxious if your friends seem to be getting replies before you do. It's not a bad sign. It could be due to all sorts of things – HEI policy and timing, number of applications received, admissions tutors' workloads, etc. You may be invited to an interview or open day first, but neither of these is automatic. Chapter 7 offers more information on interviews.

HEIs send their decisions to UCAS, whose staff pass them to you. You can log on to Track at any time to check your offers, using your Personal ID from your Welcome Letter and the same username and password you used in Apply. If you gave UCAS an email address, they will send you an email to let you know that there is some new information on your Track.

STEVE WATTS, ENGLISH LECTURER AND ADMISSIONS TUTOR, HOMERTON COLLEGE, CAMBRIDGE

'After the interviews, the interviewers meet to compare notes and make their lists of students to whom they would like to offer places. The discussions can last for hours. Normally there will be agreement over the students we are sure of. It is equally easy to agree on the ones who will not get offers. The middle band is the problem - when you have a limited number of places left and too many students in the category. We do our best to agree and give each one a score. However, we then wait for the Pool list to become available and look through the applications of some well-qualified candidates who have not been made offers by other colleges *in case we find some who have higher scores than some of our own middle band ones. In a normal year we make offers to a fairly high percentage of Pool candidates.'*

You are likely to get a letter from the HEI as well. This may arrive before or after the offer appears on Track. An offer is only valid when you receive notification from UCAS.

Offers by HEIs can be:

- U: unconditional. This means you have met the entry requirements and the HEI is happy to accept you (usually only if you already have your grades)
- C: conditional. A conditional offer will specify the conditions which you must meet to get the place. This could be in terms of UCAS tariff points or exam grades. The grades could specify a subject (or subjects) too e.g. an A in English.

And of course, the HEI decision could be a rejection (see p. 122).

Offers can come at any time, but HEIs are asked to stick to the UCAS timetable. The dates for 2011 entry are shown in Table 10.

TABLE 10.   UCAS TIMETABLE

If you applied to UCAS . . .	You can expect decisions by . . .
by 15 January 2011	6 May 2011
between 16 January 2011and 30 June 2011	19 July 2011

Although you are notified of decisions by UCAS, it is not involved in any of the decision-making process. If you have any questions about the time taken to make a decision or whether you should have heard from a particular HEI, you need to contact the HEI and not UCAS.

REPLYING TO OFFERS

You do not have to reply to any offers until you have had replies from all your choices. But there is still a deadline. Your deadline depends on when you receive your *last* offer. The dates for 2011 entry are shown in Table 11.

TABLE 11. YOUR DEADLINES FOR DECIDING ON COURSES

Last decision received by . . .	Your reply deadline is . . .
31 March 2011	5 May 2011
6 May 2011	7 June 2011
10 June 2011	30 June 2011
19 July 2011	26 July 2011

So in each case you have some time (but not limitless time) to consider your decision before you reply. When you have received all your decisions, your reply date will be shown on Track.

If you are in the lucky position of having received several offers you will now need to decline some. Other applicants may now be offered the places you decide not to accept.

You reply to the HEI decisions through Track. For each offer you receive you can choose:

- F: firm acceptance (one only)
- I: insurance acceptance (one only)
- D: decline.

Firm acceptance

You can only have one firm acceptance. At this stage, this needs to be your first choice of all your offers, i.e. the HEI where you will go if you meet the conditions of the offer (which usually involves your grades).

Insurance acceptance

You can make one insurance acceptance if you wish. This insurance choice acts as a back-up for your firm acceptance; you will need to consider your insurance option carefully – see below for some advice on this.

Decline

When you have decided which offers to accept, you have to decline the others.

MAKING YOUR DECISIONS

These are difficult decisions affecting your future, which is why UCAS gives you time to make them. This may give you time to visit the HEI or attend an open day, if you haven't already.

Your firm acceptance needs to be your first choice from the offers you receive. It does not have to be the HEI which has been your first choice all along, as may not have been offered a place at that HEI or on the course that you really wanted. Or you may have changed your mind. Since you made your UCAS choices, you may have done more research on the HEIs and courses or attended open days or interviews as well as talking to teachers and advisers. What you do need to be sure of is that your firm choice is the course you want to study in the place you want to spend the next three or more years.

It is also important to bear in mind that when you firmly accept an offer you are making a commitment to that HEI. This is the course that you are likely to end up studying if you get the grades in the offer. If you get the grades for both your firm choice and your insurance choice you cannot make the decision about which to go to. The HEI makes the decision for you and you will find that your insurance choice is automatically declined. (More about this in Chapter 9, which deals with results).

But you also need to bear in mind that you may end up at your insurance choice. So think carefully which one this should be. When you made your original UCAS choices, you chose up to five from thousands of courses at hundreds of universities. With luck, all your choices were places where you could imagine yourself being – and for courses you could imagine yourself studying. At this stage, several weeks or months later, when you are accepting and rejecting offers you need to be sure that you do not make any insurance choice unless you are certain that you would be happy on that course at that HEI.

The ideal situation is to keep as your firm choice the course that you most want to study and keep as your insurance choice a lower offer, in case you don't get the grades for the firm choice. However, as we know, life doesn't always work out like this. What happens if all your offers are the same? Maybe the course you really want to do is making a lower offer than any others?

An insurance choice doesn't have to be a lower offer than the firm choice. Your insurance choice can be any of your offers. It could even be based on higher grades than your firm choice – you may decide to do this because you would still rather go to your firm choice. Fair enough, but you need to be aware of the possible risks. If you don't get the grades, you could end up in the situation where your firm choice doesn't offer you a place – and neither does the insurance offer. So you may end up without a place, or having to find one through Clearing.

You don't have to keep an insurance offer. But, again, if you only keep a firm choice and you don't get the grades, you are likely to end up without a university place.

Some students find themselves in the lucky position of having several offers. If the offers are all for different grades, it can be tempting to accept a high offer as the firm choice and keep the lowest offer as the insurance choice. For example, the offers might be AAB, BBC and CCC. So the student keeps the AAB as the firm choice and the CCC as the insurance choice, thinking 'I'm safe. I will get these grades easily.' At results time they achieve BBC and immediately wish they had hung on to the BBC as the insurance. Adjustment was introduced to deal with this. Chapter 9 has more about Adjustment.

You can see how important – and how difficult – these decisions are. The factors you take into account are very personal, so what suits one person may not suit others. You can ask for guidance from advisers, teachers, family and elsewhere and discuss it with your friends. Ultimately, though, the decision is yours – and yours alone.

You may find it difficult to decide which offers to accept: which should become your firm choice and which your insurance choice. But you will have to make the decision – and record it on Track before the deadline.

Declining offers

When you are sure that you are making the right decision and know which is to be your firm choice and which (if any) your insurance choice, you can decline any other offers – again, using Track.

It may, of course, be the case that you decide to decline all your offers. You may have good reasons for doing this – perhaps the offers you get are too high and you (and your teachers) feel that you are unlikely to get the grades.

REJECTIONS

Instead of getting an offer from an HEI you may, of course, get a rejection. It's always disappointing, but it may happen. After all, at some point you may reject some HEIs too. There are many reasons why any of your HEIs might reject you – perhaps, for example, because your predicted (and/or actual) grades are not high enough. The reason may not even be anything about you – it may purely be that there are too many applicants for the course (so some people will inevitably have to be rejected).

What happens if you don't get any offers? Or if you receive some but decide to decline them? You may then be able to use Extra.

USING EXTRA

Extra is for people who aren't holding any offers. This may be because:

- they didn't get any offers from HEIs
- they rejected all their offers.

Rather than leave you without any possibility of a place, UCAS allows you to apply for another course which still has vacancies. To be eligible for Extra you need to have:

- received decisions from all your choices
- either had no offers or declined all the offers you have received

but *only* if you used all five choices in your original application. (Extra is also offered to CUKAS applicants with no offers.)

If you are eligible for Extra, UCAS will notify you on Track. Extra is available from the end of February to the end of the first week in July (from 25 February to 6 July 2011 for 2011 entry).

You then need to look in Course Search on the UCAS site, which will show an 'x' next to courses that still have places. UCAS suggests that before you apply you try to contact the HEI to make sure that they will consider an application from you.

When you have chosen the course, enter it in Track. UCAS will send your application to the HEI. You will be notified of an offer in the same way as before.

You need to accept or decline the offer through Track. Once you accept the offer, you are then committed and cannot apply anywhere else.

If you are not made an offer within 21 days or decide to decline one that is made, your Extra button will appear on the screen again and you may make a different choice – if Extra is still open. Remember, Extra closes at the beginning of July – 6 July 2011 for 2011 entry.

If you decide to use Extra, it is important to consider your options realistically while you are looking for vacant places. You do not have to choose the same course or subject as your original UCAS choices. You may want to look at related courses or something a bit different from your original choices. Remember that you don't have to do this alone. This really is the time to talk to your teachers, tutors and advisers.

You may want to apply for a place on a less popular course, particularly if you suspect that the reason you got no offers was that your predicted grades weren't high enough. In which case, looking at a different course or a slightly different subject may be the right thing to do – as long as they still fit in with your career plans.

You also need to decide whether you are applying for a place you really want – or are you just applying so you have a chance to go somewhere? (Because all your friends will be off to uni . . .) You need to think carefully about the HEI you are applying to as well as the subject and course. The point I made earlier in the section 'Making your decisions' is just as relevant here, so here's a reminder:

> **Bear in mind that you may end up at your Extra choice of HEI, so you need to be sure that you would be happy on that course at that HEI for the next three or more years.**

There is another option to consider. You could wait and apply through Clearing instead (Clearing is available after exam results are published to help those left without an HEI place – there's more on Clearing in Chapter 9). Why might you want to do this? Because there will be more places available through Clearing than through Extra. At results time, many applicants are holding a firm choice and an insurance choice. As the results are published, for each applicant at least one of the places they are holding will become vacant – sometimes both, if they don't get the grades for either choice. Some of the places that are now vacant may be on some of the 'top' courses which you might prefer to some of the 'unwanted' vacancies on Extra.

If you do use Extra, but still end up without a place by July – either because you weren't offered a place or you declined those you were offered – then you can still use Clearing.

There are no guarantees with any of this. Places *may* become available – but no one can know for sure at any stage, whether in Extra or in Clearing, which places will be there for you to apply for. Do they sound like difficult decisions? They are! Again, you are not alone as you consider your options. Your teachers, tutors and advisers will have helped people through this process many times before. When facing difficult choices you may not want anyone to tell you what to do (it's your life), but it can really help to talk over the options with someone else.

EXTRA TIPS

- Be prepared to be flexible.
- Perhaps choose a different course . . .
- . . . Or an HEI you had not previously considered.
- Consider all your options.
- Think about whether using Clearing might suit you better.
- Get help and advice from your teachers, tutors or advisers.

CHAPTER NINE
RESULTS DAY

The results of summer exams are published in July or August. International Baccalaureate (IB) results come out at the beginning of July, Scottish exams in early August and A levels later in August. Dates for 2011 exams are:

- IB: 5 July
- Scottish exams: 4 August
- A levels: 18 August.

As A levels are the latest set of exam results to be published (as well as the largest group), HEIs wait until the A level results are published to confirm offers being held. Generally, you will find out whether or not you have a place on results day.

It is important to be available at results time, as you may have to make some decisions quickly. It's not a good time to be out of the country, for example. Yes, you can log on to Track from anywhere with an internet connection – and this is fine if your results are good and you've got the grades you need for one of the choices you are holding. Track will tell you that your place is confirmed. However, if your results are disappointing, you will have to decide whether you want to look for vacant places through Clearing – which often involves contacting HEIs by phone. If your results are excellent you may want to use Adjustment to look for an alternative (better?) place. (There is more on both Clearing and Adjustment below.)

It's not impossible to deal with Clearing or Adjustment if you are away from home, but not necessarily straightforward (or cheap). Neither is it feasible to nominate someone to do this on your behalf. You need to be around to speak to HEIs personally and make the decisions that will affect you for at least the next three years.

Schools and colleges differ in how they let students have the results, though most nowadays invite students to come in on results day. Rather than getting your results through the post – and perhaps having to wait for delayed post – going in to school or college means you can share your results with your friends. You can congratulate each other on successes and support each other through disappointments.

Because UCAS Track is available 24 hours a day, some people log on before they go to school to collect their results so they know whether they have a confirmed HEI place. Others prefer not to do this – they would rather find out their results at school, with their support system available to share the news. The staff, too, will want to be part of your results. They have been teaching you through your exam courses – some of them may have known you for seven years if you have stayed at your secondary school for sixth form. They want to share your successes too.

But just as importantly, the staff are there to help you if your results are disappointing, particularly if this means you have not got the grades you need for your firm choice of university place – even more so if your results mean that you have ended up without a university place at all. It does happen. When the results came out in 2010, it was estimated that nearly 180,000 people ended up without a higher education place. Some of these were people with top grades, including the new A*.

Many schools and colleges have advisers on hand on results day – usually teaching staff along with advisers from the local careers or Connexions service. They are there to support you as you make decisions based on your results.

UCAS receives the exam results before you do. This may seem unfair – they're your results after all, based on your hard work. But you can imagine what a massive task it is for the HEIs and UCAS to look at all the results and match them to everyone's firm and insurance choices and work out who has achieved their grades and who hasn't.

When you have your results, your next move is to log on to Track to find out whether you have been accepted by either your firm or your insurance choice.

Generally, if you meet or exceed the grades required by your firm choice you will be accepted. If not, but you meet the grades for your insurance choice, you will be accepted. If you haven't quite met the grades for either choice, either or both may still decide to accept you. This is why it's important to look at Track as well as getting your results.

If you are accepted, what do you need to do on results day? Not much! Just celebrate and be glad that all your hard work paid off – and perhaps be on hand for any of your friends who haven't done so well. UCAS will send you a confirmation letter in the post. This is the official notification of your HEI place.

There is no need to contact the HEI admissions staff at this stage. In fact if you do, you are likely to find they are too busy dealing with applications through Clearing.

WHAT IF YOU DON'T GET THE GRADES?

As mentioned above, if you've nearly met the grades required by an HEI in a conditional offer, they may still offer you a place on the course you originally applied for.

In some cases, the HEI may offer a place on another course – in UCAS, this is known as a changed course offer. The offer may be for a related subject or a different qualification – a BSc in Engineering rather than BEng, or an HND rather than a degree. This is intended as a serious offer by the HEI, but remember they have places to fill on their courses. It may be a less popular course and therefore harder to fill. If you are serious about wanting to get on one of the best courses, then a different qualification may not suit you – and your career plans. You need to give any offer careful consideration. UCAS gives you five days to reply to a changed course offer.

If neither of the offers you are holding turns into a confirmed place then you are automatically entered into Clearing. This allows you to apply for any places which are now vacant. Remember that many of the places that are being held – as both firm and insurance choices – will have become available when offers are confirmed.

Clearing

You will be eligible for Clearing if one of the following applies (provided that you haven't withdrawn your application):

- you are holding no offers
- your offers have not been confirmed (i.e. you have not met the conditions of a conditional offer)
- you have declined your offers or have not responded by the due date
- your offers have not been confirmed and you have declined any alternative offers from the same university or college
- you applied after 30 June.

Clearing offers a real chance to get a place at a top HEI. In 2009, over 47,000 students found a place through Clearing. Some universities, including those in the Russell Group, even keep back some places to offer in Clearing. They are hoping to pick up some of the top candidates – that could be you!

JOE STATHERS-TRACEY, HEAD OF THEATRE AND PERFORMANCE DESIGN AND THEATRE AND PERFORMANCE TECHNOLOGY AT LIPA

'We occasionally have a few places available after results day – or late applications. We will do a telephone interview. Sometimes these are people with an unusual education background. Many turn out to be very good candidates.'

You need to be aware, though, that some top courses will not be available through Clearing. Oxford and Cambridge, for example, do not take part. Other courses find they do not need to.

JONATHAN HOGG, ADMISSIONS OFFICER, SCHOOL OF HISTORY, UNIVERSITY OF LIVERPOOL

'We don't usually need to go into Clearing.'

KIERON SALMON, DIRECTOR OF ADMISSIONS, THE SCHOOL OF VETERINARY SCIENCE, UNIVERSITY OF LIVERPOOL

'We do not usually take part in Clearing. If we find ourselves with any places after the results are out, we contact candidates from our interview list and offer them a place.'

Clearing opens for places in HEIs in Scotland on Scottish results day (4 August 2011 for 2011 entry). So, if you are interested in applying for a place at a Scottish HEI only, this may interest you. But if you want to look at UK-wide vacancies you will have to wait for the full UK Clearing service to open on results day.

How does Clearing work?

You need to use Track (as UCAS will not send you a letter at this stage to tell you if you are eligible for Clearing). If you are eligible, an 'Add Clearing choice' button appears. Track will tell you your Clearing number – which HEIs will ask for when you contact them.

Clearing vacancies are displayed on the UCAS website and in the *Independent*. You can also phone the UCAS helpline. So the first thing to do is search for vacancies. You don't have to stick to any of the original choices you made. You can look for different subjects and look at different HEIs. But you can also apply to any of the HEIs which turned you down earlier in the process.

What you will need to do is act quickly. Although there are thousands of places in Clearing the number of students is much higher – in 2010, over 180,000 students were chasing about 32,000 Clearing places. Particularly in the early stages of Clearing, the situation changes rapidly as places are filled and others become vacant.

If you are serious about wanting a place through Clearing you will have to devote a lot of your time to the process, particularly on results day and over the next few days.

When you find vacancies which interest you, the next stage is to contact the HEI. You can approach as many HEIs as you like. In fact, if you find several Clearing vacancies which interest you, is it a good idea to contact each HEI at this stage. They all have Clearing helplines, with staff ready to deal with you. They will tell you whether places are indeed available (the situation changes so rapidly that places may have filled while you were waiting to get through on the phone) and may be able to offer you a place.

The HEI will ask for your Clearing number, which they can use to look at your original UCAS application. At some HEIs, the helpline staff pass you through to the relevant academic department where, again, staff are ready to deal with you. Academic staff may interview you briefly over the phone. They will want to know that you have a real interest in the course you are applying for. They may also discuss with you related courses or subjects if they think these might suit you better.

The HEI can make you a provisional offer over the phone. If you want to be formally considered for this place, you must use the 'Add Clearing choice' button and enter the course details. The HEI gives you a date by which you must do this. It is important to realise that offers made over the phone are only provisional. They will have made provisional offers to many other callers too.

The HEI will confirm or decline your application. If you are declined, the 'Add Clearing choice' button will be shown again and you can apply for another place.

Applying through Clearing can be hard work – both in terms of time and your emotions. You've probably already had the upset of not getting the grades you needed. Just at the time when you are dealing with this disappointment, you have to keep a clear head and start making some decisions. However you are feeling, it really is worth acting swiftly.

Although it is important to act quickly, it is just as important to do your research. Just as you did when you were making your original selection of HEIs for your UCAS application, you need to find out as much as you can about any new courses or HEIs you apply to through Clearing. As you know, HEI websites are full of information. You may even want to visit the HEI before you decide. Many HEIs have open days for Clearing applicants.

You could visit the HEI (and/or the local town) before you add that HEI as a Clearing choice or while waiting for them to make a decision. There may not be much time to organise a visit to an HEI, but it is feasible. The process of UCAS passing your Clearing choice to the HEI, the HEI making a decision and passing that back to UCAS to display on Track can take a few days. As results day is a Thursday, your first applications and decisions are likely to be on Thursday or Friday, so you could visit at the weekend.

In deciding whether or when to visit, you will need to consider:

- how sure you are that you want to go to this HEI from the information you have already
- that other people will have provisional offers and may turn these into applications before you do
- whether visiting one HEI is the best use of your time. Would you be better staying at home to research other vacancies and contact other HEIs?

. . . as well as practical considerations, such as how far away the HEI is and your other commitments in those few days (e.g. whether you have a job).

If you are at school on results day, your teachers, tutors and advisers will help you start the Clearing process. They may be able to make suggestions about alternative courses or HEIs for you to consider. If you don't have internet access at home, then your school or college may make this available for you.

You can see now why it's best not to be away from home at this time. Getting your results, logging on to Track and contacting HEIs may not be easy from your tent at a festival! During Clearing, admissions staff will want to speak to you personally to discuss vacancies.

JAMES GOT HIS PLACE AT QUEEN MARY, UNIVERSITY OF LONDON THROUGH CLEARING

'I worked really hard for my A levels so I was pretty sure I could get the AAB grades I required for my offer. On results day when I found out I'd got ABC, I was devastated. I didn't know what I should do. It felt as though all my plans had gone out of the window and all that hard work had been for nothing. At first, I wasn't really interested in Clearing as I felt it would only have all the places which no one else wanted. On the day after results day, I'd calmed down enough to have a look at what was available. Some of the places were at universities which I hadn't considered before. I didn't want to go somewhere just to get a university place so I was careful where I applied to. When I saw that Queen Mary had places on engineering courses, I phoned them. They made me an offer for Materials Science and Engineering, which was quite different from the Civil Engineering that I'd applied for. I had a lot of thinking to do about whether I wanted to do something so different. Although I had a few days, I felt under pressure to make the right decision.

'I applied for the place on Friday and had to wait over the weekend to see if the offer was confirmed. By this time, I'd looked a bit more at the Queen Mary website to see exactly where in London it is and what the facilities are like - I wanted to go somewhere I could keep up my rugby. I liked what I saw. So I accepted their offer. All this took about five days. At the time, it felt quite stressful, but looking back, I'm surprised how easy it was. I've ended up going where I wanted to go (London) on a really good course. I'd never thought about doing Materials Science, but I'm finding it interesting.'

WHAT IF YOUR GRADES ARE HIGHER THAN YOU EXPECTED?

Of course, your results might be better than you expected – or better than any of your HEIs were expecting. You may end up with much higher grades than your firm choice. You might wish you'd chosen a different course (or HEI). Since 2009, UCAS has run a facility called Adjustment, which allows students in this situation to hold on to their confirmed place while they look for another one.

How does Adjustment work?

You are not entered into Adjustment automatically (unlike Clearing). You have to register for Adjustment in Track if you want to use it.

Adjustment opens on results day (18 August 2011 for 2011 entry). Your individual adjustment period starts at the point when your conditional firm choice is confirmed on Track. From then you have a maximum of 120 hours (five complete 24-hour periods, including Saturdays and Sundays) to find another choice. Adjustment ends on 31 August, so if you register after 27 August you will have less than five days. Your Track will show when your Adjustment period finishes.

You are only eligible for Adjustment if your results have met and *exceeded* the conditions of your firm choice. This includes any specific conditions, such as getting a certain grade in a particular subject. So, for example, if your offer was

- ABB (A in English) and you got ABC (with A in English) you would not be eligible

or

- if your offer was BB and you got BBC you would not be eligible.

You would be eligible if, for example, you received an offer of ABB and you got AAB.

If your original offer was unconditional, you cannot use Adjustment. You cannot use Adjustment on your insurance choice either.

Adjustment gives you a last chance in this application cycle to try for a place on a top course. You need to bear in mind, though, that competitive courses may be full already. However, you may feel it is worth a try, especially if your results are a lot better than your offer.

You will need to get in touch with the admissions staff at the HEI. Try to contact the relevant department if you can. Make it clear when you phone that you are applying through Adjustment. Staff may ask for your Personal ID so they can access your UCAS application – they will want to see your Personal Statement and reference as well as talking to you. Be prepared to talk about why you have chosen this course and why you are a good candidate.

In a sense, you have nothing to lose – if you cannot find a place through Adjustment you are still accepted at your original confirmed place.

DIFFERENT PLANS?

It is a fact that not everyone who applied for an HEI place will get one. Even if you go through Clearing you may still end up without a place. While you are going through the UCAS application process, it is a good idea to think about what you might do if this happens to you. You may never need these plans, but if you do, you will be glad you've considered your options in advance.

Retakes and re-applying

One of your choices is to apply again through UCAS next year. If your application is based on your current grades, any offers will be unconditional, which takes much of the uncertainty out of the application process.

You could decide to retake your exams to try for higher grades. This might seem like the option for you if you had set your sights on a top course. But retakes aren't the right choice for everyone – you may not want to do all that studying over again. But if you really want to get on that course it might be what you have to do.

You need to find out from admissions staff on your chosen course whether they have a policy on retakes. This can vary – some places really don't want applications from those who needed to take the exams again to get good grades, while others see it as a positive sign of your determination to get on the course. There may be some indication of this on the HEI website – or, more likely, on the department's web pages. (This sort of policy is likely to vary from department to department.) It is worth making contact with the department and expressing an interest in what you need to do to get that place you really want.

Re-applying gives you the chance to spend the year doing something else. Depending on your frame of mind, you could see this as an opportunity or as an unnecessary delay in the progression of your plans. Some of your options for a year off (gap year) could include:

- working: to earn money and/or to gain experience relevant for your studies
- travel: for pleasure or, again, it could be relevant for your course
- volunteering: another way to gain relevant experience
- further study: as well as retakes, another GCSE, A level or vocational course may strengthen your application next time.

If you have ended up without a place because you had no offers from any of your UCAS choices, you need to try to work out why this was. If you had interviews, you may be able to get some feedback about your application.

In some cases, there are specific things you can address. For example, if one of the entry requirements for the vocational course you have applied for is to have some relevant work experience, you could increase the quantity – or, more usefully, the quality – of your related experience.

KIERON SALMON, DIRECTOR OF ADMISSIONS, THE SCHOOL OF VETERINARY SCIENCE, UNIVERSITY OF LIVERPOOL

'Candidates can ask for feedback – they have to apply in writing. We will give them feedback about their application in terms of their interview, work experience or grades. We will tell them whether they gave a strong, weak or average performance. We are happy to see people re-apply, as long as they have addressed the reason why they failed.'

JONATHAN HOGG, ADMISSIONS OFFICER, SCHOOL OF HISTORY, UNIVERSITY OF LIVERPOOL

'We are more than happy to see people re-apply. In fact, we quite like it as it shows they are motivated. Resits are fine too.'

Through all of this, it is important that you are realistic. There is no point in aiming for a course that is beyond you. However, if you have a burning ambition for a particular course (and the career that it leads to), then you will want to work hard to achieve it. The people who know you and your abilities will be able to help you decide what is realistic. You will need to re-examine your career plans – again, to check that your ambitions are realistic for you. And that, of course, is what's important. You are not fulfilling anyone else's career ambitions but your own. Because this is all about your career plans. Getting on a top course at one of the best universities is only the start.

Once you've looked again at your career plans, you may, of course, decide to consider other options apart from higher education. This doesn't mean turning your back on higher education for ever. You can apply through UCAS at any age. It is possible that if you wait a year or more, you may have more idea of what you want to do or more motivation to study. And, of course, if you apply in future you will already have your results. This takes much of the uncertainty out of the application process, as any offers will be unconditional.

Here are a couple of examples of students who weren't successful with their first applications, but got onto the course in the end – one was successful the second time and the other on her third attempt!

MARIA IS A STUDENT AT THE SCHOOL OF VETERINARY SCIENCE, THE UNIVERSITY OF LIVERPOOL

'I think if you're determined you can and will do it. I wanted to be a vet ever since I was six and was able to diagnose what was wrong with my pet hamster. Despite working in a local veterinary practice after school for two-and-a-half years and helping on a farm with the lambing, I was rejected when I first applied and the feedback was about my work experience. I spent the year in between broadening my experience, with large animals in particular. So the second time I applied I was successful.'

ESTHER IS AN ACTING STUDENT AT LIPA

'I now realise I wasn't ready for the LIPA experience when I first applied. I was rejected without even getting an audition. So I went away and started an apprenticeship with a theatre company. I also worked as a special needs teaching assistant. I learnt a lot from both experiences - and I grew up a lot. The second time I applied I had an audition but didn't get accepted. Applying several times made me more focused. The first time, I had applied to ten or eleven drama schools. At my second attempt, I applied to three, but by the third time, I knew I wanted to study at LIPA so I only applied there.'

Other options

Of course higher education isn't the only option open to you after Year 12 or 13 (S5 or S6 in Scotland). In the section above, I mentioned some of the possibilities if you decide to take a year out. Some of the suggestions may seem OK on a temporary basis, but are not really a sustainable long-term option – travelling, for instance, may not be possible for any length of time without money to live on.

If you've been ambitious in your higher education plans, you are likely to continue to have high aspirations. What are the alternatives to higher education which might live up to your ambitions? You might want to look into:

- A level training schemes
- apprenticeships
- jobs
- internships.

A level training schemes

You may be aware of graduate training programmes for those with a degree. In fact, that may be what you were aiming for after your higher education. But you may not know that some large organisations positively welcome young people onto training programmes after A levels/Highers, too. Typical entry requirements are 180 UCAS points across any subjects, together with good GCSE/Standard Grades. The programmes are intended to train future managers – they are often called something like trainee management programme.

The website www.notgoingtouni.co.uk specialises in this type of vacancy. Other vacancies for these programmes are advertised on company websites, so it's worth doing some research using your usual search engine.

A quick trawl showed current vacancies in:

- retail management
- finance management
- estate agency/property valuation
- IT
- accountancy.

All A level training programmes train you within the organisation itself. Often, they involve working in different departments of the organisation to broaden your experience. All include opportunities to gain qualifications – the best are based round a recognised qualification such as a Foundation degree or professional exams.

Apprenticeships

An Apprenticeship might suit you, particularly if you were thinking of studying a vocational subject in higher education. Apprenticeships offer the chance to train for a particular occupation by combining relevant qualifications with practical training in the workplace (something which not all higher education courses offer).

You may associate Apprenticeships with those who leave school at the age of 16. Think again! Did you know that Apprenticeships are available at different levels? Three levels, in fact:

1 Apprenticeships

2 Advanced Apprenticeships

3 Higher Apprenticeships.

(In Wales, they are referred to as Foundation Apprenticeships and Apprenticeships and in Scotland as Modern Apprenticeships. In Northern Ireland, the ApprenticeshipsNI prgramme covers all levels).

All Apprenticeships, at whatever level, combine work and training. Each includes a range of qualifications. Some are directly related to the Apprenticeship – NVQs, BTEC Certificates and Diplomas, etc. – and others are more general, such as qualifications in leadership. All these qualifications can be 'topped up' to a higher level, including degrees. All Apprenticeships pay a training allowance or a salary.

Some Advanced Apprenticeships require applicants to have at least one A level. For example, the Young Scientist Advanced Apprenticeship requires chemistry A level and includes studying towards a part-time degree in applied chemistry. Other Advanced Apprenticeships set their minimum entry requirements at GCSE level, but in practice many entrants have already studied to A level or beyond.

Advanced Apprenticeships are available in many career areas. Here are some examples:

- accountancy
- fundraising manager
- information and library services
- livestock or animal care
- project designer (construction)
- public relations officer
- stage manager
- team leader
- veterinary nurse.

You will notice that several have 'manager' in their title, indicating that the training will be for positions of responsibility.

Some job areas also offer Higher Apprenticeships, which combine work – often in a leadership role – with a higher level of qualifications – NVQ 4 or a Foundation degree. Examples include:

- accounting
- aerospace engineering
- business analyst
- IT.

Many Apprenticeship vacancies are advertised on the following websites:

- www.apprenticeships.org.uk (England)
- www.apprenticeshipsinscotland.com (Scotland)
- www.nidirect.gov.uk/apprenticeshipsni (Northern Ireland)
- http://new.careerswales.com/16to19 (Wales).

Some employers advertise them on their own websites and others are advertised in the local or national press.

Jobs

You may decide to go straight into work – after all, you'll need something to live on and contribute to household expenses. However, the current (2011) economic climate may narrow your choices for finding a job. You may end up taking a job in, say, a shop or bar just to tide you over. In the short term, that may well be a realistic strategy, but probably not what you had in mind for yourself. However, even if a job doesn't fit in with your ambitious career plans, you will still be gaining valuable skills. Chapter 10 outlines the 'transferable' skills which every employer is looking for at whatever level.

You can develop your transferable skills in any job. For example, in bar or shop work you'd be developing your teamwork, communication skills and commercial awareness. But a job which fits in with your career plans would be even better. How about:

- administration in a solicitors practice if your plan included law?
- childcare work if you were planning to become a social worker?
- working with older people if you were hoping to do medicine?

At least then, while you decide whether or not to re-apply for higher education, you are gaining valuable relevant experience to add weight to a future application.

Internships

If you are determined to carry through your ambitions, you may want to get direct experience of your chosen career area. In some occupations, this is very difficult through actual paid work – mainly because of the numbers trying to enter such areas as:

- media
- fashion
- advertising.

Internships are also available in other career areas, however.

Internships have become a recognised way of entering some professions (with or without a degree). You need to be aware, though, that internships are unpaid, so this may not be the right option for you for any more than a short period.

Several websites offer internship vacancies. It is worth bearing in mind, though, that there is little difference between an 'internship' and any other kind of work experience, placement, work shadowing, etc. – all are unpaid and each contributes to your portfolio of experience to present to HEIs or future employers. There is no reason, therefore, why you can't take steps to arrange your own internship/placement. You could then decide for yourself how long (or how many hours a week) you wanted it to be – and negotiate accordingly with the employer.

As pointed out in Chapter 4, relevant work experience that you have researched, found and arranged for yourself is going to be even more impressive than just applying for an advertised vacancy.

A FINAL NOTE

If you are dealing with disappointment after unexpected results, you may find this encouraging: the University of Oxford, in *Oxford Interviews* (downloadable from www.ox.ac.uk/admissions/undergraduate_courses/how_to_apply/ interviews), makes the point that even though those who apply are on the whole the most academically successful at their school or college, 75% of applicants are turned down. It goes on to offer encouragement by saying that almost all go on to study elsewhere and that many decide on further study at Oxford, so they often see unsuccessful undergraduate applicants returning as postgrads.

CHAPTER TEN
LOOKING AHEAD

WHEN YOU GRADUATE

his book is about gaining a place on the course you want. But it pays to look ahead as well . . .

Having a degree from a high-status HEI is not necessarily enough! You will be very lucky if you can move straight into a top job even with a good degree from one of the best universities. It is an increasingly competitive world, with more and more graduates competing for what is currently (2011) a very tough job market.

The first consideration is that most employers specify they are looking for graduates with a *good* degree. Usually this means a 2:1 or above, so this is what to aim for during your studies to have any realistic chance of success as a graduate. As well as specifying which class of degree, employers may also look back to A level, Higher or diploma results and ask for minimum grades, certain grades in particular subjects or a minimum number of UCAS points. For example:

- one international management consultancy asks for at least 340 UCAS points (AAB or equivalent – not including general studies) and a predicted (or obtained) 2:1 degree
- a national retail group requires a good degree in any subject.

As you can see, some jobs are open to students with degrees in any subject. More than this, many employers encourage applications from a wide range of graduates in different subjects. It's not that employers are necessarily interested in your in-depth knowledge of eighteenth-century political history or Shakespeare's plays. As well as the intellectual capacity demonstrated by degree-level study, employers are looking for what are known as soft or transferable skills. These are personal skills that can be transferred to most working environments. They sit apart from the knowledge you acquired during your degree but some of them may have been developed during your course – time management as you juggle work and play, working together on collaborative projects for assessment and written communication skills from all those essays and assignments.

When the Institute of Directors surveyed 500 directors in 2007, 64% said graduates' employability skills are more important than occupational, technical or academic knowledge/skills associated with the degree. The current economic climate is likely to make this even higher.

What are transferable skills?

There are many surveys asking employers which skills they are looking for in graduates (as well as other applicants for jobs). These are the ones that keep cropping up time and time again:

- ability to cope under pressure
- adaptability
- commercial awareness
- communication, both verbal and written
- initiative
- leadership
- numeracy
- persuasion skills
- problem-solving ability
- self-reliance
- teamwork.

Obviously, many jobs do require a specific degree subject. However, employers in these areas also look for the above qualities. Engineers, accountants and scientists, for example, need to be able to lead, manage, communicate and work with other people.

Here are some more examples from job ads on a graduate jobs website.

HM Revenue and Customs

- 2:1 in any discipline

National supermarket chain

- 2:1 degree or above
- Flexible with location

International energy provider

- At least a 2:2 degree in any discipline
- Real ambition and genuine commercial savvy

International IT group

- At least a 2:1 degree
- Business and technical insight
- A flair for solving problems creatively

IT consultants

- 300 UCAS points
- At least a 2:1 degree in an IT, engineering or scientific subject
- Excellent written and oral communication
- Strong team players
- Confident
- Proactive
- Able to work on their own in initiative
- Able to work alone
- Able to manage many work streams in parallel

Improving your employability

Chapter 2 talked about employability. Although this is increasingly part of many higher education courses, it is always worth using your own initiative to increase your transferable skills. If you can get a job or placement which is relevant to your chosen career path this will be an obvious benefit – and for vocational courses this is often a requirement and therefore arranged by or through the HEI. Any paid work can be useful though – and not only for the money! Like many students, you may end up working in a bar or shop. You will still be developing skills from the list above, such as teamwork, communication, problem solving and so on.

Employers are always interested in paid work experience. However, you can develop your employability skills in other ways. Some may be obvious, such as voluntary work or internships. But many of your student activities will be of interest to employers, as they will develop or demonstrate transferable skills. Here are some other examples:

- sports: determination, teamwork
- societies: organisational skills
- events: communication, budgeting, teamwork
- student union: persuasion skills, leadership.

So, however much you are determined to enjoy your time in higher education – and who can blame you? – it's worth keeping one eye on the future. And, for most people, the future is sooner or later likely to involve the world of work.

FURTHER INFORMATION

I nevitably, there is so much information, especially on the internet, that it helps to be pointed in the right direction. Each HEI has its own website – far too many to list – and, within that, each school, department or faculty has a section. Here are some other useful websites.

ADMISSIONS TESTS

www.admissionstests.cambridgeassessment.org.uk
www.lnat.ac.uk
www.ukcat.ac.uk

APPLICATIONS

www.ucas.com
www.cukas.ac.uk

LEAGUE TABLES

www.thecompleteuniversityguide.co.uk
www.thegooduniversityguide.org.uk (access restricted to *The Times* online subscribers)
www.gurdian.co.uk/education/universityguide

STATISTICS

www.hesa.ac.uk
www.hecsu.ac.uk
www.hefce.ac.uk
www.rae.ac.uk
www.thestudentsurvey.com
http://unistats.direct.gov.uk

STUDENT SITES

www.studentuk.com
www.thestudentroom.co.uk
www.uk-student.net

OTHER

www.prospects.ac.uk
www.russellgroup.ac.uk

OTHER OPPORTUNITIES

www.apprenticeships.org.uk
www.apprenticeshipsinscotland.com
www.nidirect.gov.uk/apprenticeshipsni
http://new.careerswales.com/16to19
www.notgoingtouni.co.uk

TELEPHONE NUMBERS

UCAS Customer Service Helpline (Monday to Friday, 08:30–18:00)
0871 468 0468
CUKAS Customer Service Helpline (Monday to Friday, 08:30–18:00)
0871 468 0470